Spectrum

Spectrum

Heritage Patterns and Colours

Introduction by Ros Byam Shaw

With 117 illustrations

 Thames & Hudson |

Introduction	6	About this book	12
15th century	14		
16th century	22		
17th century	30	About these objects	13
18th century	52		
19th century	82		
20th–21st century	140		
		Further reading	254
Acknowledgments	255	Picture credits	255

Preceding pages: Textile design for L. Galy, Gallien et cie, 1762, gouache and ink on paper, France, T.408-1972

Left: Pattern book by unknown artist/maker, 1750–1850, possibly France, T.59-1922

Introduction
by Ros Byam Shaw

The Victoria and Albert Museum, London, is a repository of some of the finest, rarest and most beautiful examples of human creativity in all areas of the decorative arts. Its collection of fabrics for interiors includes medieval tapestries, Renaissance embroideries, Persian carpets and Indian chintzes, coming right up to date with 21st-century designs you might still buy to decorate your own home. Wallpapers, increasingly popular and affordable from the late 18th century onwards, are also well represented.

The V&A was created with inspiration as much as education in mind. Its forerunner, the Museum of Manufacturers, was established in 1852, prompted by the huge success of the Great Exhibition of 1851. Despite, or perhaps because of, the popularity of this magnificent show of extraordinary products, displayed and housed in the glittering giant vitrine of the Crystal Palace, many of those most closely associated with its planning and organization were concerned by what they rather patronizingly regarded as the 'bad taste' of the general public. As an antidote to the brash, machine-made consumer goods increasingly available to an ever-wider, and very eager, clientele, Prince Albert and Henry Cole decided that a permanent collection showcasing 'the design works of past and present to provide inspiration for designers and manufacturers, and to influence the taste of the general public' was necessary. Both would approve of a book that offers examples from the collection in a way designed not only to delight but also to inform with its innovative dissection of colour ingredients.

The 115 detail images of patterned textiles and wallpapers selected for this book are like cherries picked from a huge bowl of delicious fruit. Presented in chronological order, the earliest detail is taken from an embroidery of 1400–30 in brick red, dusky pink, sage green, mustard yellow and smoky blue (pages 16–17), the last from a graphic wallpaper design of 2009 that combines orange and mustard yellow on a dramatic, dark background (pages 252–3). Next to each pattern is a colour grid, which shows the relative proportions of the most prominent colours used, each labelled with its CMYK number – a worldwide standard printing method for colour that precisely identifies it. These grids offer a way to look at the component colours – their balance and weight, and their effect in combination – without the distraction of the patterns they comprise.

As you turn the pages, the cumulative impression is dazzling. From the densely peopled, fabulously detailed hunting tapestry of the early 15th century (pages 18–19), to the charming geometry of stylized pomegranates on a 17th-century Turkish domestic embroidery (pages 32–3), to the 19th-century printed cottons thick with brightly coloured, accurately drawn garden flowers, here is a sample book showcasing generations of skill and artistry. Chosen for their beauty and verve, rather than as typical examples of their date and origin, this array of patterns nonetheless represents a visual history, albeit a fragmented one, of an important aspect of interior decorating: the various ways we have chosen over the centuries to embellish our homes.

The first third of the book covers the period from 1400 to 1800, with the remaining two-thirds of the book devoted to works of the 19th, 20th and 21st centuries. It is easy to forget, from our privileged modern position of infinite choice, just how time-consuming and difficult it once was to create colour, let alone pattern. Ready-mixed household paints, for example, have only been available since the beginning of the last century. And it was only in the late 19th century that chemical dyes made from coal-tar – which, conveniently at a time of gas lighting, was a waste product of gas manufacture – were developed for use on fabrics, offering both a wider and much cheaper range of vibrant hues for the home.

Before the Industrial Revolution, the vast majority of domestic interiors were necessarily plain and simple, with whitewashed walls, perhaps tinted with an earth pigment such as ochre or umber. Fabrics were used sparingly, and were assiduously re-used and recycled. The colour scheme was largely drab. The jewel-bright hues and rich patterns glowing on pages 16–81 were delights only available to an extremely wealthy minority. From the 15th through the late 18th century, when they fell out of favour, tapestries were some of the most valuable – and therefore most ostentatious – possessions. Still hanging in the original space for which they were commissioned, the Abraham tapestries in the Great Hall of Hampton Court, woven in wool and silk and incorporating miles of gold and silver wrapped thread, cost Henry VIII

£2,000, a vast sum at the time that could equally have bought him two fully equipped battle ships. The natural dyes – weld for yellow, madder for red, woad for blue – have faded and the metal threads have tarnished, but they must once have glittered and flared with a magnificence that justified their stupendous expense.

There is a huge gulf between the manufacturing methods of these rare, precious early pieces, made from yarns gathered and spun by hand and dyed using pigments that had to be meticulously prepared, and modern digital printing, which can reproduce any image in any number of colours on fabric, paper, leather – or even plastic designed to be mounted on the side of a lorry. Despite this gulf, and the fact that early vegetable dyes were unstable and have often faded beyond recognition, the pages of this book show a surprising number of links between designs of the past and the present, as motifs and colour combinations regularly reoccur, a reminder of how ancient and pervasive are the habits of nostalgic revival and international borrowing.

Long before modern globalization, when communication between continents took months and years instead of microseconds, patterns were being shared and copied. Turning the pages, and travelling back through the centuries, what is striking is not so much the progress of history, but its circularity. Black backgrounds are one of the more noticeable colour tropes, the black background of a medieval *millefleurs* tapestry (pages 20–1) recurring in a 17th-century embroidered hanging from Turkey (pages 42–3), an 18th-century English needlepoint embroidery (pages 60–1), a late 18th-century textile design (pages 74–5), a Walter Crane wallpaper of 1897–8 (pages 134–5) and a Collier Campbell cotton from 1974 (pages 236–7). Equally apparent is the enduring popularity of red and green used together as the dominant colour theme of a design – still noticeable, despite the fact that the yellow dyes of the past, which were added to woad or indigo to make green, have often disappeared leaving the more stable blue behind.

Red and green, in their many shades ranging from pink and sage to crimson and emerald, are complementary colours, found opposite one another on the colour wheel, which places the three primary colours – red, yellow and blue – at equal distances, with the secondary and tertiary colours mixed from them in the spaces between. (The other well-known pairing of complementary colours is yellow and blue, which, in this selection at least, is less prevalent.) The colour wheel is one of the more simple ways to map colour; there are more complex colour models that take into account variations of tone (how much grey has been added), tint (how much white has been added) and shade (how much black has been added).

As for motifs, there are multiple echoes and repeats, across time and across the world: the sinuous necks of mid-19th-century embroidered cranes from Japan (pages 102–3) mirrored by herons and swans in a design of 1939 by Edward Bawden (pages 206–7); the wavy parallel stems of a 17th-century Turkish cushion cover (pages 44–5) reimagined as centipedes in a velvet by Timorous Beasties in 1992 (pages 246–7). Pomegranates pop up several times, from 17th-century Turkey to late 19th-century Britain. The perennially popular paisley teardrop, formed of flowers on a curved stem and originating in Persia, appears in a 19th-century design for a lining fabric from Iran (pages 84–5), and transformed into a bird in a furnishing fabric of the 1960s (pages 230–1). Realistic or stylized, flowers and birds have rarely been out of fashion.

Fashion does intervene, of course: affected by technical innovations; or by trade, as in the mid-18th century craze for Chinoiserie; or by new discoveries, as in the Renaissance reclamation of classical idioms, or the excavations of Pompeii and Herculaneum in the second half of the 18th century, which added colour to the Neoclassical repertoire. Even tax has its role: heavy duties, such as those imposed in 18th-century Britain on wallpapers, chintzes from India and woven silks from France among other things, had the effect of making these items more rather than less covetable, their expense equated with luxury and exclusivity.

Meanwhile, fashion has its own momentum as the slow swing of the pendulum between extremes of what historian and curator Peter Thornton described as 'density' – a collective taste for rooms that are more, or less, busy and full – affects how much colour and pattern in a room is seen as elegant and desirable. Inevitably, this last effect is not apparent in a book that privileges pattern and colour. The trend towards abstraction in designs for interiors, however, reflecting the movement away from figurative art, is obvious in the selection of fabrics and wallpapers from the first decades of the 20th century. Culture and religion also have their part to play, whether the Islamic tendency to exclude images of people and animals, or in the symbolism of the natural world that is integral to the aesthetic of Japan.

Over the centuries there have been various concerted attempts to suppress pattern and colour. The Puritans finished the job of whitewashing richly decorated church interiors that had begun in the Reformation. More recently, Modernism, with its disapproval of ornament – 'a needless expression of degeneracy' as Adolf Loos so tartly put it – has successfully disseminated its doctrine of white walls and straight lines. Fortunately there is something joyful and life-affirming about colour and pattern that refuses to be quashed. They keep bobbing up again, catching our eyes like twinkling lights in a dark sky, intriguing our brains.

Aside from enjoying its richness and variety, how might a creative reader use this gorgeous compendium? Leafing through it, certain combinations may have particular appeal: colours set against a neutral ground, for example, such as an English embroidery of the early 17th century (pages 38–9), and the Josef Frank printed cotton of c.1930 (pages 182–3). A glance at their colour grids reveals that the neutral shade is the majority shareholder, and that each design contains a further six colours, including shades of red, green and yellow. In the earlier fabric the colours have a more even distribution, but in the Frank a vibrant cobalt blue predominates. A translation into a colour scheme for a room could use the neutral for the walls and floor and the brighter colours for curtains and upholstery. If taking the Frank as a template, that might suggest a sofa in cobalt blue, and cushions in terracotta and lime green. This sounds dauntingly garish, but a look back at the fabric reveals how well these colours harmonize. Alternatively, the fabrics with black backgrounds might conjure visions of walls in inky blue, or charcoal grey as a theatrical foil for paintings and furnishings, just as the fabrics with red backgrounds could prompt ideas for a red carpet or rug.

After more than thirty years spent looking at, and thinking and writing about, domestic interiors, I have come to realize that there are few, if any, hard and fast rules that cannot be broken. The best designers and decorators add instinct and intuition to their experience and knowledge, and often find inspiration in the most unexpected places. This book contains more than a hundred colour palettes, any one of which could spark an idea for decorating a single room or a whole house, for a fresh design for a wallpaper or fabric, or even for an outfit. But, as you can see from the patterns they are taken from, a colour palette is only the beginning.

About this book

The V&A collection is a treasure trove for the visitor interested in colour and pattern. At Here Design we were given complete freedom in making the pattern selection for this book, and narrowing it down has been no mean feat. Ultimately, aside from intellectual considerations of time and place, we chose patterns that simply *felt* exciting, interesting, or unusual to us. So much about colour is subjective! As designers who are lucky enough to work with colours day in and day out, however, we like to think we've acquired a certain sensitivity to, and expertise on, the subject.

When drawing simple palettes from often complex patterns, we considered coverage of physical space, as well as optical prominence, to determine the proportions of colours. The modular grid on which the palettes are built allows us to express those ratios, although not with mathematical exactitude.

Some palettes are limited to three or four colours; others would have had dozens, had we not exercised judgment in rationalizing the relevant shades. Once a selection was made, we used software to extract colour values from the digital photography of each item (already colour-corrected against the real object in the museum). With this technique, the colours in the palettes truly represent the colours in the patterns, even though it may not always seem that way!

Our intention was for this book to be both a compendium of beautiful patterns for inspiration and a functional tool. We labelled each swatch with its CMYK value: this is a standard system for specifying printed colours, based on varying percentages of cyan, magenta, yellow and black inks. Unfortunately, no printer is perfectly accurate, so there may be minor variations between the appearance of swatches in this book and the shade obtained by reproducing the same values with a different printer or in another medium. While every effort has been made to match the tints accurately, the swatches do not replace professional colour-matching systems such as Pantone or RAL.

About these objects

The objects from the V&A collection sourced for this book have been titled according to their general use, if known. In cases where a fabric may have been used for several purposes, for clothing or furnishing, we have simply called this a 'textile'. 'Panel' indicates that a length of fabric was combined with others to create a whole.

As this book is a celebration of details of pattern and colour, most of the images in the following pages show only a small portion of the object or pattern. To learn more about a pattern in the context of the complete object, please consult the V&A website at www.vam.ac.uk, where you can search the collection using the museum accession number that appears at the end of each identification caption.

15th century

C26 M93 Y100 K25

C20 M26 Y76 K5

C31 M28 Y78 K11

C23 M57 Y65 K13

C51 M41 Y60 K31

C51 M29 Y28 K8

C21 M35 Y54 K9

C11 M14 Y23 K1

Book cushion cover 1400–30

Unknown artist/maker

Linen embroidered with silk and edged with silk cord

Germany

1324–1864

During the Middle Ages the church was an immensely important patron of weaving and embroidery. Book cushions were used to prop up liturgical books on the altar during services to protect the valuable books from wear and tear while in use. This particular piece of embroidery may have been part of a portable or house altar. It shows the Virgin and Child seated under a canopy, with St Joseph bearing a basket in one hand and a lily in the other. The group is flanked by angels.

The Boar and Bear Hunt
Tapestry
1425–30

Unknown artist/maker

Tapestry woven with wool warp
and weft

Netherlands

T.204-1957
Accepted by HM Government in lieu of tax
payable on the estate of the 10th Duke
of Devonshire and allocated to the Victoria
and Albert Museum

Tapestries with hunting subjects were
popular throughout the 15th and early
16th centuries. Hunting was not only a
practical activity but also a focus of
elaborate rituals integral to court etiquette.
The hunters in this piece wear elaborate
court dress, typical of the Burgundian court
in the 1420s, and the flowers and trees
in full foliage suggest perpetual spring.
Tapestries were often used to decorate
and to help insulate a complete chamber.
They would have hung from floor to ceiling,
placed edge to edge like wallpaper in a
modern home. Few of this age and size,
at almost 4 × 10 m (13 × 32 ft), have
survived centuries of use.

15TH CENTURY

C18 M81 Y75 K7

C58 M29 Y36 K10

C33 M24 Y54 K7

C45 M71 Y71 K70

C19 M20 Y38 K3

C75 M38 Y63 K31

C28 M68 Y87 K25

C19 M46 Y70 K7

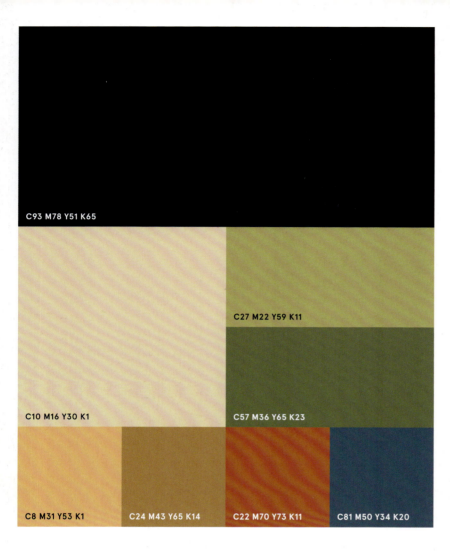

C93 M78 Y51 K65

C27 M22 Y59 K11

C10 M16 Y30 K1

C57 M36 Y65 K23

C8 M31 Y53 K1

C24 M43 Y65 K14

C22 M70 Y73 K11

C81 M50 Y34 K20

Tapestry
*c.*1500

Unknown artist/maker
Tapestry woven in wool and silk
Flanders

232-1894

This is a fragment from what may have been a larger tapestry hanging. It is a type known as *millefleurs* ('a thousand flowers'). This popular style from the late 15th and early 16th centuries is associated with northern France and Flanders. *Millefleurs* tapestries often included small animals and birds among the flowers, such as the partridges and cock shown here, and sometimes featured the owner's coat of arms, in which case the animals might be symbolic. The unicorn was associated with chastity and invulnerability, since legend held that only a virgin might catch and tame it.

16th century

C17 M86 Y55 K6		
C21 M27 Y84 K7	C64 M36 Y91 K25	
	C75 M57 Y37 K26	
C19 M73 Y37 K6	C15 M40 Y24 K2	C58 M33 Y28 K9	C24 M23 Y35 K4

Panel
1560s

Unknown artist/maker

Silk in satin weave, embroidered
with silk

France

T.219B-1981

This panel probably formed part of a decorative bed valance. The embroidered imagery illustrates the romance of Pyramus and Thisbe from Ovid's *Metamorphoses*. It is quite likely that it derives from a pattern book of designs. Such books were increasingly available from the early 16th century onwards and professional embroiderers would adapt the published designs to suit their own tastes. The embroidery is exceptionally skilful and executed in the grotesque style of decoration fashionable at the time. It is possible that this panel was made for Catherine de Medici (1519-89) or another member of the 16th-century French court.

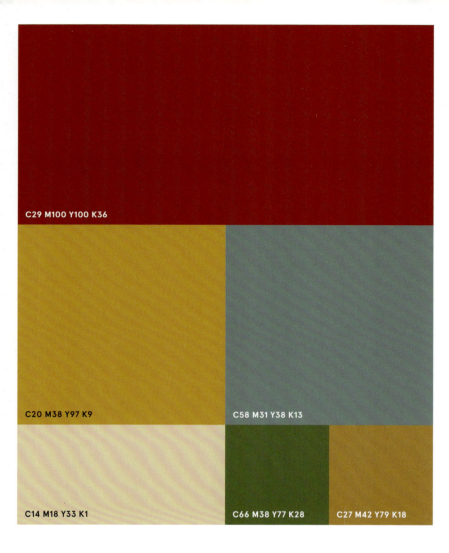

C29 M100 Y100 K36

C20 M38 Y97 K9

C58 M31 Y38 K13

C14 M18 Y33 K1

C66 M38 Y77 K28

C27 M42 Y79 K18

Hanging
1580–90

Unknown artist/maker

Felted wool, applied silk
and silk cord

England

T.209-2004
Supported by the Friends of the V&A

This striking late 16th-century textile,
with its design of a lattice of scrolls
containing Tudor roses, was probably
part of a wall hanging. A small number
of appliqués with a woollen ground
survive, but no other example of this
type with this particular combination of
materials and style of decoration. It is not
exceptionally luxurious or sophisticated,
however, and may have been the work
of skilled amateur embroiderers. As such,
it would have been appropriate for the
rooms of a noble family or the walls
of a merchant's house.

C33 M39 Y54 K21

C10 M22 Y58 K1

C20 M24 Y32 K4

C62 M54 Y82 K61

C46 M36 Y59 K21

C30 M57 Y97 K28

C31 M96 Y87 K43

C64 M41 Y32 K15

Hanging
Late 16th to early
17th century

Unknown artist/maker

Silk velvet and metal-wrapped thread

Iran

T.226-1923
Purchased with the assistance of
The Art Fund, Mr I. Schwaiger, Selfridge
& Co. Ltd., Mr A. F. Kendrick, Mr O. S.
Berberyan, G. P. & J. Baker Ltd. and
Mr A. Benardout

Silk textiles decorated with large human figures are one of the most striking products of Iranian weavers in the 16th and 17th centuries. This length of velvet was probably used as a wall hanging. It shows aristocratic young men standing in a flower-strewn garden, flanking a cypress tree that grows by a fish pond. In silk pile and silver, on a gold ground, this is a masterpiece of velvet weaving.

17th century

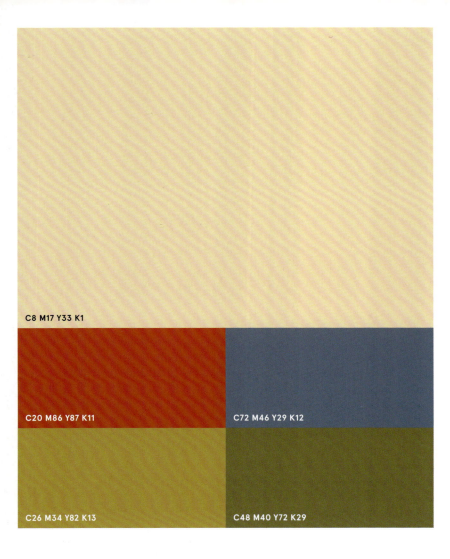

C8 M17 Y33 K1

C20 M86 Y87 K11

C72 M46 Y29 K12

C26 M34 Y82 K13

C48 M40 Y72 K29

Hanging or cover
17th century

Unknown artist/maker
Linen embroidered with silk
Turkey

CIRC.92-1953
Given by Miss Ethel C. Newill

The designs of domestic embroideries like this one, typically made by women in their own homes, are based on the more expensive woven silks popular at the Ottoman court. The embroideries have the same flowers, serrated leaves and other motifs that appear in woven silks, but their shapes are often less well defined. Large panels served as quilt covers and hangings. Smaller pieces were used as napkins, sashes and towels, or for wrapping possessions for carrying to the public bath. Most of the embroidery is done in simple stitches such as darning stitch, couching and running stitch.

C73 M68 Y56 K74

C16 M27 Y89 K4

C28 M94 Y79 K31

C19 M52 Y92 K8

C70 M37 Y62 K26

C16 M69 Y71 K5

C68 M36 Y42 K21

C15 M14 Y45 K1

Carpet
1600–25

Unknown artist/maker
Hand-knotted wool and cotton pile,
on silk warp and cotton weft
Iran

T.131-1926

This is a fragment of the right-hand
border of a Persian carpet dating from
the late 16th or early 17th century.
The beautiful confronting birds are not
quite symmetrically positioned within
their cartouche, and each bird is slightly
different. It indicates that the weaver
was working from a sketch; the birds
would have been identical if a cartoon
had been used.

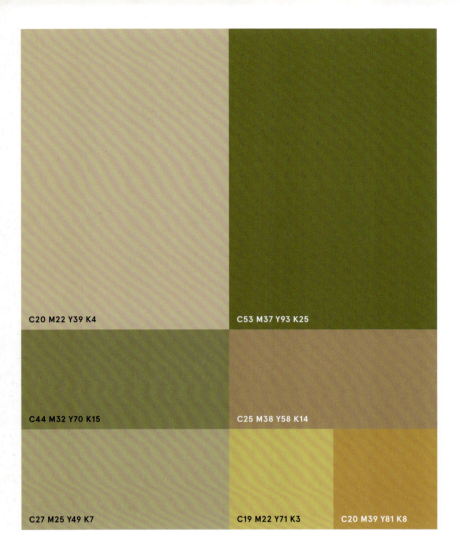

C20 M22 Y39 K4

C53 M37 Y93 K25

C44 M32 Y70 K15

C25 M38 Y58 K14

C27 M25 Y49 K7

C19 M22 Y71 K3

C20 M39 Y81 K8

Textile
1600–29

Unknown artist/maker
Woven silk
Italy

1027-1888

The production of patterned silk textiles in the 17th century required considerable investment in equipment and raw materials, and the skills of artisan weavers; consequently, there were relatively few centres of production in Europe. The majority of luxury silks, probably including this example, were produced in the Italian city-states. This floral repeating pattern has affinities with the so-called *jardinière* polychrome floral velvets produced in Genoa that were prized as formal interior furnishing fabrics.

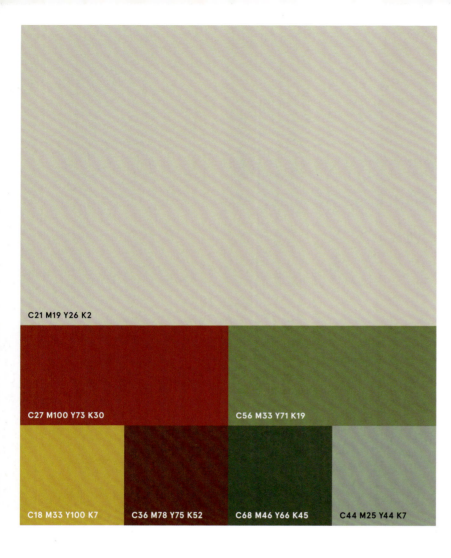

C21 M19 Y26 K2

C27 M100 Y73 K30

C56 M33 Y71 K19

C18 M33 Y100 K7

C36 M78 Y75 K52

C68 M46 Y66 K45

C44 M25 Y44 K7

Hanging or cover
1600–30

Unknown artist/maker
Linen embroidered with silk
England

T.396-1988
Given by the Descendants of the Storeys
of Lancaster

This embroidered linen hanging or cover has a repeating all-over pattern of red holly berries in groups on curving green branches interspersed with stylized holly leaves, all rendered using both outline and fill-in stitches in various shades of green, red, silver and gold silk. This form of all-over pattern was the most typical English embroidery design of the period. A variety of coiling plants decorated household textiles such as towels, table and cupboard cloths, and coverlets and pillows, as well as linen dress accessories.

C14 M84 Y45 K4

C9 M23 Y83 K1

C45 M36 Y80 K23

C9 M17 Y54 K1

C4 M4 Y4 K0

C23 M58 Y91 K13

Textile
1600–49

Unknown artist/maker
Brocaded silk satin
Italy

T.360-1977

Brocaded polychrome silks like this piece were luxury items in the 17th century. This panel is made of silk with a satin ground, brocaded with metal thread and vividly coloured floss silk. The technique of brocading, which creates a raised pattern on the face of the fabric, made it possible for silk weavers to create more naturalistic and detailed decorative motifs, such as the lively birds in this design.

C66 M60 Y63 K74

C22 M91 Y99 K15

C15 M39 Y92 K4

C65 M41 Y81 K35

C46 M29 Y45 K11

C9 M11 Y35 K1

Hanging
1600–99

Unknown artist/maker
Linen embroidered with silk
Turkey

T.62-1916
Given by Lady Church

The oldest Ottoman embroideries in the V&A date from the 16th or 17th centuries. They are either whole covers and wall hangings or fragments of them. They are decorated with large-scale, bold designs in red, blue, green and yellow, with some white and black. In the 17th century the main designs were based on wavy parallel stems that run along the length of the fabric. The black ground of this embroidery is very unusual.

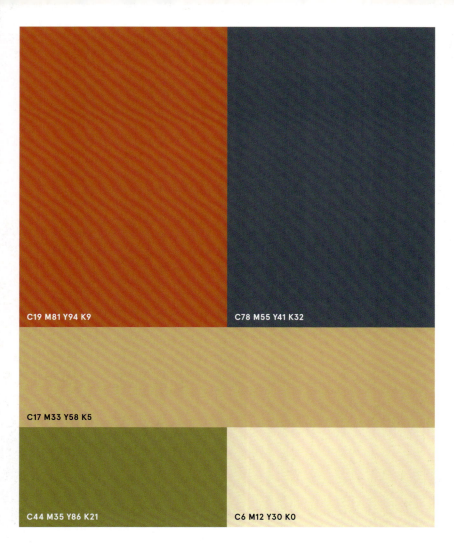

C19 M81 Y94 K9

C78 M55 Y41 K32

C17 M33 Y58 K5

C44 M35 Y86 K21

C6 M12 Y30 K0

Cushion cover
1600–99

Unknown artist/maker
Linen embroidered with silk
Turkey

T.129-1928

This linen cushion cover is embroidered in silk with a design of stylized leaves, stems and flowers. It is a lovely example of the popular 17th-century Ottoman pattern of wavy parallel stems – in this case, thick blue stems decorated internally by a red line with small white flowers and pomegranates. Alternating from the left and the right of these stems are large red leaves, each containing a green stem with blue and white flowers: a carnation, tulips and pomegranates.

C28 M99 Y89 K34

C22 M38 Y76 K11

C13 M14 Y28 K1

C50 M67 Y50 K59

C37 M96 Y77 K61

C46 M18 Y24 K2

C19 M73 Y48 K7

Tapestry
1600–99

Unknown artist/maker

Tapestry woven in wool
on cotton warp

Peru

T.15-1923
Given by Louis C. Clarke

This tapestry panel is woven in coloured
wools on cotton warps. In the middle is
an ecclesiastical hat with four tassels
surmounted by a mitre. On one side is a
crozier and a glove and on the other an
archiepiscopal cross and biretta. The rest
of the red ground is filled with animals and
birds in pairs, including hummingbirds and
parrots, flowers and detached leaves. There
is a triple border filled with continuous
foliage at the upper and lower ends.

Cushion cover
1640–70

Unknown artist/maker

Linen canvas embroidered with
wool and silk

England

443-1865
Given by H.F.C. Lewin

This embroidery depicts scenes from
the Old Testament story of Abraham and
Isaac, a very popular subject in English
17th-century domestic embroidery. It was
worked as the front of a cushion cover
by an accomplished amateur embroiderer.
The design would have been drawn on the
canvas in black outline by a professional
pattern drawer, adapting published prints.
The embroiderer's individual taste could
dictate choice of colour and, to a more
limited extent, stitch and type of thread.
This embroidery was never made into an
object for use, which is one reason that
its colours are still so bright.

C13 M47 Y54 K2

C20 M26 Y88 K6

C93 M58 Y34 K20

C29 M45 Y85 K21

C54 M27 Y87 K10

81 M54 Y57 K61

C78 M37 Y66 K30

C20 M82 Y93 K11

C49 M18 Y38 K3

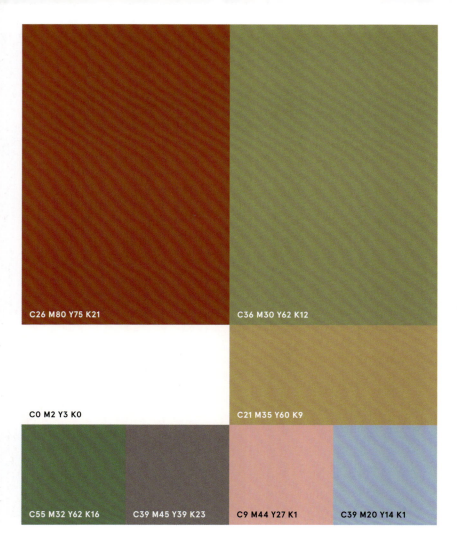

C26 M80 Y75 K21

C36 M30 Y62 K12

C0 M2 Y3 K0

C21 M35 Y60 K9

C55 M32 Y62 K16

C39 M45 Y39 K23

C9 M44 Y27 K1

C39 M20 Y14 K1

Tent hanging
Late 17th to early
18th century

Unknown artist/maker
Block-printed, painted
and resist-dyed cotton

India

IM.29-1928

Decorated cloth panels were used extensively in the interiors of the tents set up for Mughal rulers and their courts when they were outside the palaces hunting or engaged in military campaigns. Several panels would be joined together to form moveable screens (*qanat*s) for privacy around the rulers' enclosures. Hangings and *qanat*s were also used inside palaces for decoration and to divide large halls into smaller spaces.

18th century

C7 M60 Y87 K1

C17 M71 Y90 K6

C24 M51 Y77 K15

C14 M22 Y92 K2

C90 M83 Y36 K32

C33 M24 Y22 K3

C27 M92 Y82 K28

C62 M51 Y95 K56

Textile
*c.*1700

Unknown artist/maker

Silk damask, brocaded in silks
and silver-gilt thread

France

T.166-1927
Given by J.B. Clarke-Thornhill

The bold pattern and distinctive colouring
of this brocaded silk date it to a brief
period around 1700 when such a
combination was fashionable. At that
time the increasing trade between Asia
and Europe greatly influenced the design
of French silks, such as this piece, which
were inspired not only by motifs on
textiles from Asia, but also by those of
imported porcelain and lacquer objects.
Books on natural history were another
source for the imagery of exotic flowers,
fruit, fish, birds and other creatures used
by European silk designers.

C3 M8 Y11 K0

C92 M80 Y60 K95

C95 M80 Y42 K44

C46 M81 Y73 K74

C10 M32 Y79 K1

C32 M78 Y75 K39

C21 M59 Y72 K10

C60 M47 Y63 K45

C22 M31 Y88 K9

Bed curtain
1700–15

Unknown artist/maker

Cotton and linen twill embroidered with wool

England

353-1907

This embroidered curtain was made as part of a full set of bed hangings. Crewelwork hangings became the most popular form of English domestic furnishing in the late 17th and early 18th centuries. Their design, typically featuring trees, leaves and trailing branches, was heavily influenced by the Indian embroideries imported by the East India Company. During the late 19th and early 20th centuries these embroideries experienced a revival and became fashionable antiques, while contemporary designers and manufacturers produced printed linens with similar designs.

C11 M16 Y22 K0

C35 M88 Y62 K31

C18 M99 Y81 K8

C50 M35 Y37 K2

C84 M63 Y46 K30

C8 M48 Y22 K0

C42 M67 Y39 K10

Palampore
1720–50

Unknown artist/maker
Cotton chintz, painted and dyed
India

IS.132-1950
Given by G.P. Baker

This palampore or chintz hanging was made on the Coromandel Coast in south-eastern India. The design of a flowering tree growing from a small mound is typical. Its bold colouring and relatively small size suggest that it was made for the Dutch export market, possibly for use in parts of Sri Lanka controlled by the Dutch East India Company. Palampores were regularly exported to 18th-century Europe, where they were valued as wall hangings and bed or table coverings.

Cushion
1730–69

Unknown artist/maker

Canvas embroidered with wool and
silk, backed with silk damask

England

T.77-1969
Bequeathed by Brigadier W.E. Clark

Canvas, often decorated with embroidery,
remained a basic material for 17th- and
early 18th-century furnishings, from
carpets and wall hangings to seats and
cushions. This cushion was made by
a non-professional, albeit skilled,
embroiderer, probably for use at home.
The flowers are depicted in a naturalistic
style that became dominant in the mid-
18th century, although earlier fashions for
Indian and Chinoiserie embroidery motifs
still persisted. The cushion is backed
with a Chinese export red silk damask
furnishing fabric.

100 M96 Y49 K71

C15 M32 Y86 K4

C20 M11 Y15 K0

C14 M44 Y24 K1

C100 M84 Y13 K1

C53 M37 Y48 K22

C22 M100 Y96 K17

C56 M41 Y29 K12

C27 M20 Y51 K4

C7 M7 Y13 K0

C9 M17 Y56 K1

C26 M41 Y67 K16

C7 M9 Y34 K0

C25 M45 Y33 K10

C7 M23 Y16 K0

C20 M73 Y52 K9

Design for a woven silk 1734

Anna Maria Garthwaite (1690–1763)
Watercolour on paper
England

5971:23

Anna Maria Garthwaite was born in 1690 and became one of the leading pattern-drawers in the English silk industry despite probably not having had the formal technical training that was usually considered necessary to take up the profession. She produced as many as eighty commissioned designs, such as this one, every year for master weavers and mercers. She lived and worked in Spitalfields, London, from about 1730 until her death in 1763. Her interest in natural forms, and her talent for depicting them, characterized her designs throughout her professional life.

C13 M83 Y81 K3

C71 M42 Y16 K2

C11 M5 Y16 K0

C13 M43 Y66 K3

C91 M83 Y36 K33

C53 M24 Y54 K7

C15 M47 Y38 K4

Panel
1740–1820

Unknown artist/maker

Silk satin embroidered with
coloured silk and gilt thread

China

FE.114-1974
Given by Dr Joan Evans

This red silk celebratory hanging was
made for an annual Chinese festival in
honour of the Weaver Girl, a celestial
maiden who influences the fate of
humankind by the pattern she weaves.
The festival, in which traditionally only
women participate, celebrates needlework
skills and the embroidery on this piece
is appropriately lavish. This detail shows
a moon on the left, in which the female
deity Chang'e stands with a white hare.
Women playing musical instruments sit
in a pavilion on the right, while those
in the centre pay homage to the Weaver
Girl who, out of sight, descends through
clouds on the back of a dragon.

C13 M15 Y21 K1

C27 M98 Y87 K27

C65 M37 Y40 K20

C26 M22 Y53 K5

C73 M51 Y50 K46

C14 M46 Y34 K2

C14 M37 Y48 K3

Coverlet or floor-spread Mid-18th century

Unknown artist/maker

Cotton hand-embroidered with silk and metal thread, and quilted

India

IM.2-1912

This delicately designed, rectangular quilted coverlet (*palang posh* in Urdu) or floor spread of undyed cotton features an embroidered central medallion, corner quarter-medallions and floral decoration in coloured silk and metal-wrapped thread. The similarities between this design and other pieces known to have belonged to the court of Tipu, Sultan of Mysore (r.1782–99) suggest that this embroidery also comes from the Deccan Plateau in southern India.

C15 M14 Y22 K1

C21 M81 Y70 K11

C18 M45 Y46 K6

Furnishing fabric 1750–90

Unknown artist/maker
Cotton, copperplate-printed
France

T.318-1919

This copperplate-printed cotton was made in Nantes, France, one of several cities that developed this textile specialism in the second half of the 18th century. Designers took inspiration from historical and contemporary literature, and from descriptions of the cultures encountered by Europeans on their travels in Asia and the Middle East from the 16th century onwards. This design represents a scene from *La vie de Gargantua et de Pantagruel*, a series of five comic novels by 16th-century satirical author François Rabelais, in which the characters visit 'Cathay', the name by which northern China was known in medieval Europe.

C27 M47 Y100 K21

C17 M66 Y32 K4

C31 M98 Y58 K40

C22 M92 Y89 K16

C68 M56 Y77 K69

C14 M31 Y100 K3

C42 M47 Y88 K40

C40 M30 Y39 K12

Pattern book
1763

John Kelly
Worsted (wool) samples,
mounted on paper
England

67-1885
Given by Mrs Bland

These patterns were sent to Spain and Portugal in 1763 by John Kelly, agent of a Norwich textiles manufacturer. Customers abroad could choose from numbered samples and have their orders prepared back in Norwich. Worsted, a woven woollen fabric, is prepared for weaving by combing rather than carding and often has a smooth finish. According to a contemporary writer, 18th-century worsteds were 'woven in various patterns ... composed of the richest and most brilliant dyes [in] an endless diversity of colours ... this manufacture was peculiar to Norwich, and the colours employed for it surpassed any others dyed in Europe'.

NB. the Figure in ye Corners
was Nº 63.

NB. the Figure in the Cent
was Nº 52.

Nº 39.

2

3

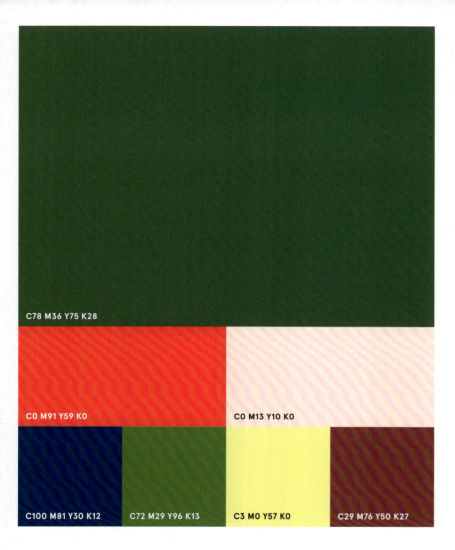

C78 M36 Y75 K28

C0 M91 Y59 K0

C0 M13 Y10 K0

C100 M81 Y30 K12

C72 M29 Y96 K13

C3 M0 Y57 K0

C29 M76 Y50 K27

Textile
1770–80

Unknown artist/maker

Plain-weave silk with hand-painted
decoration

China

T.121-1933
Given by J. Gordon Deedes

In the 18th and early 19th centuries
imported hand-painted silks were
popular in England for both dresses
and furnishings. They were rarely at
the height of fashion, however, because
their decoration often went out of style
during the long voyages from East Asia.
Nevertheless, they remained long-term
favourites with British customers from
about 1780 to 1830 because they were
pretty, exotic and relatively inexpensive.

C84 M71 Y56 K72

C51 M31 Y69 K14

C23 M27 Y77 K7

C37 M48 Y74 K36

C22 M10 Y6 K0

C15 M43 Y3 K0

C38 M90 Y54 K60

Design for a textile
*c.*1788–92

William Kilburn (1745–1818)
Watercolour on paper
England

E.894:112/1-1978
Purchased from the funds of
the Capt. H.B. Murray Bequest

William Kilburn was a talented designer who created drawings and engravings as well as many original textile patterns. He specialized in botanical subjects and presented a muslin chintz printed with one of his delicate seaweed motifs to Queen Charlotte. Sadly, his designs were often pirated within weeks of their appearance on the market. Rival firms would print the same designs with fewer colours on cheaper cloth and sell them at two-thirds the cost of the original. Despite a successful petition to Parliament in 1787 to protect his copyright, Kilburn's business was damaged and he went bankrupt in 1802.

C33 M13 Y40 K1

C73 M16 Y67 K2

C22 M34 Y32 K7

C22 M76 Y56 K13

C23 M12 Y28 K1

C65 M50 Y55 K49

C28 M23 Y76 K6

C37 M27 Y30 K7

Wallpaper
1790–1820

Unknown artist/maker
Ink and watercolour on paper
China

E.2848-1923

The upper part of this Qing dynasty
wallpaper is decorated with flowering
branches of camellia. The lower part
(not shown here) depicts a tea-making
ceremony amidst scenery including tea
houses, pagodas, rock gardens and water.
This wallpaper is said to have been given
to a former owner of Shernfold Park, Kent,
by a Chinese ambassador.

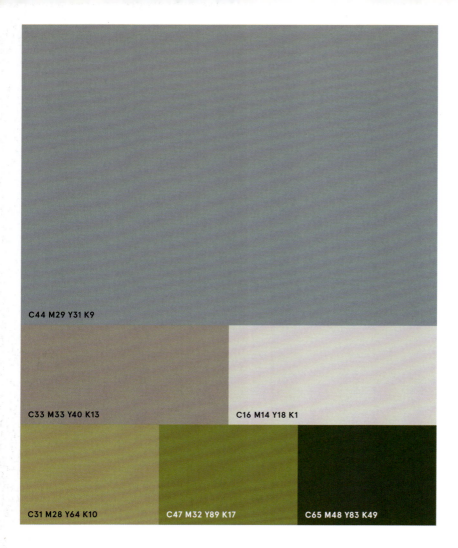

C44 M29 Y31 K9

C33 M33 Y40 K13

C16 M14 Y18 K1

C31 M28 Y64 K10

C47 M32 Y89 K17

C65 M48 Y83 K49

Furnishing fabric
*c.*1797–8

Probably Jean-Démosthène
Dugourc (1749–1825)

Woven silk brocaded in
silver thread

France

T.69-1951

This luxurious brocaded silk in the
Neoclassical style was manufactured
by Camille Pernon et Cie in Lyon.
An archived sketch of the pattern from
1797 is annotated, 'probably made for
Carlos IV of Spain'. Pernon et Cie sent
designer François Grognard to advertise
its work to the Spanish court and began
to receive commissions in 1787. Spanish
royal patronage helped the firm to survive
the loss of former aristocratic patrons after
the 1789 French Revolution. The style
of this piece is in keeping with others
designed by Jean-Démosthène Dugourc,
notably those hanging in the Billiard Room
in the Casa del Labrador in Aranjuez.

C24 M33 Y53 K10

C26 M85 Y87 K23

C76 M58 Y44 K40

C44 M41 Y56 K29

C22 M60 Y59 K11

C38 M64 Y58 K51

Tent hanging
Late 18th century

Unknown artist/maker

Block-printed, painted
and dyed cotton

India

IS.131-1950
Given by G.P. Baker

The design of this painted, printed and
dyed cotton hanging is derived from the
classic Mughal motif of a flowering tree
set within an arch. Its relatively late date,
however, and the fact that it was produced
in south-east India rather than in a north
Indian centre of Mughal culture, imply
that the design has taken on a new form.
The border is typical of textiles made
around Masulipatam, north of Madras
on the so-called Coromandel Coast.
The motif of the flowering plant emerging
from a tiny vase is similar to that seen on
other south Indian tent hangings made
for Tipu, Sultan of Mysore (r.1782–99).

19th century

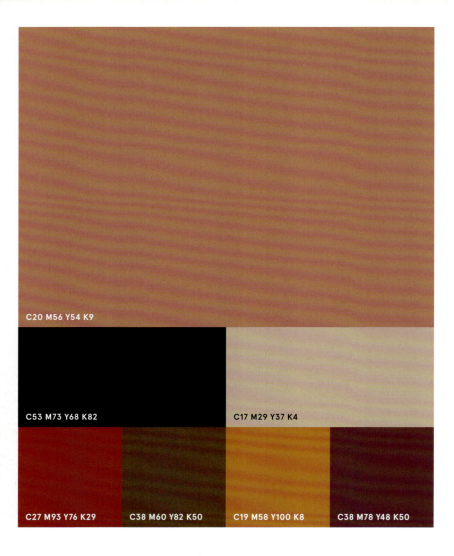

C20 M56 Y54 K9

C53 M73 Y68 K82

C17 M29 Y37 K4

C27 M93 Y76 K29

C38 M60 Y82 K50

C19 M58 Y100 K8

C38 M78 Y48 K50

Cover backing 1800–60

Unknown artist/maker
Plain-weave block-printed cotton
Iran

503-1874

This printed cotton was chosen as a decorative backing for a quilted and embroidered mat or cover. It features a very popular design motif consisting of flowers on a short, curving stem with an indication of roots below. This motif has the same profile as the Persian *boteh* (variously translated as 'bush', 'shrub' or 'cluster of leaves') from which Western paisley textile designs derive. The piece was purchased in Tehran in 1873, as part of the V&A's first large acquisition of Iranian textiles, ceramics, metalwork and inlaid woodwork.

C18 M34 Y95 K6

C24 M87 Y88 K20

C56 M56 Y55 K57

C62 M39 Y74 K29

C64 M48 Y43 K33

Textile sample
1800–1950

Unknown artist/maker
Cotton, silk and hemp
Ryukyu Islands

T.142-1968

This Ryukyuan fragment is taken from an album of fifty-two mounted textiles decorated with a variety of woven and resist-dyed patterns. It is an example of *kasuri*, a technique in which threads are selectively pre-dyed, the pattern emerging as the fabric cloth is woven. The archipelago of the Ryukyu Islands, particularly the southern Okinawa Islands, has a rich tradition of textile craft and production. Colour pigments for dyeing were traditionally extracted from subtropical plants growing locally, including turmeric, which creates a vibrant yellow dye.

19TH CENTURY

C64 M50 Y63 K54

C19 M94 Y99 K9

C10 M37 Y73 K1

C4 M11 Y0 K0

C76 M49 Y0 K0

C57 M87 Y50 K81

Furnishing fabric 1808

Unknown artist/maker
Block-printed cotton
UK

CIRC.244-1956
Given by the Calico Printers' Association

From 1800 to 1820 the finest printed furnishing textiles were polychrome woodblock-printed cottons. This fabric might have been used for curtains, upholstery, or both, as it was fashionable in this period to match the pattern on different furnishings within a room. The hatched red and blue ground was, unusually for a furnishing print, created in the 'lapis style'. This printing technique, developed in France and England, depends on the use of a resist-red that acts as both a mordant for madder dye and a resist for indigo (mordants allow certain dyes to release their colours, while resists prevent others from fixing to the cloth).

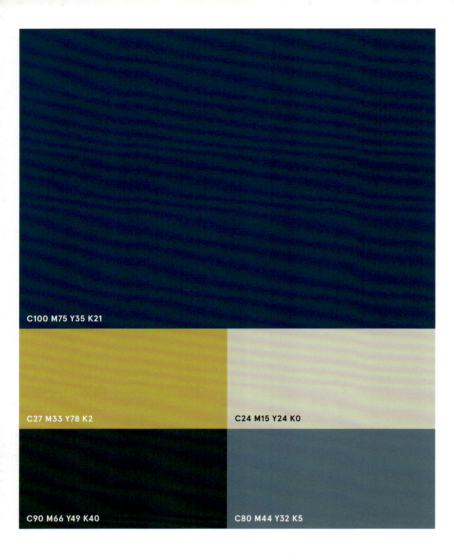

C100 M75 Y35 K21

C27 M33 Y78 K2

C24 M15 Y24 K0

C90 M66 Y49 K40

C80 M44 Y32 K5

Furnishing fabric 1826

Samuel Matley & Sons
Roller-printed cotton
UK

CIRC.271-1956
Given by the Calico Printers' Association

In 1783 Thomas Bell of Glasgow patented a process for printing textiles with engraved metal rollers. The circumference of the roller limited the height of the repeat but the process was fast, and cheaper than block or copperplate printing techniques. In the 1820s and 1830s metal rollers became more elaborate and were sometimes intricately engraved to produce minute, fancy patterns. Samuel Matley & Sons made fabrics for the lower and middle-grade domestic and export markets. This design features a Corinthian column with acanthus scroll.

C15 M19 Y37 K0

C87 M67 Y15 K2

C22 M75 Y52 K4

C19 M39 Y74 K1

C44 M36 Y75 K10

C13 M13 Y13 K0

Furnishing fabric 1830

Unknown artist/maker
Roller-printed cotton
UK

CIRC.295-1956
Given by the Calico Printers' Association

Areas of solid colour were commonly added to roller-printed textiles using wooden 'surface' rollers. In the 1830s the technique was still new and manufacturers struggled to obtain accurate prints. Some parts of the dark yellow on this textile have not registered correctly: the dark yellow beak of the parent bird in the lower left, for example, has been printed to one side. The chrome yellow dye used in this piece was one of the new generation of mineral colours that transformed the palette of 19th-century textiles from about 1817.

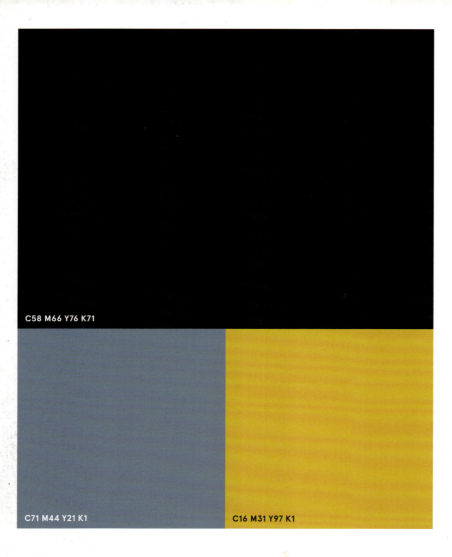

C58 M66 Y76 K71

C71 M44 Y21 K1

C16 M31 Y97 K1

Furnishing fabric 1831

Unknown artist/maker
Roller-printed cotton
UK

CIRC.293-1956
Given by the Calico Printers' Association

The detailed and naturalistic birds depicted on this fabric derive from John James Audubon's exquisite illustrations for his ground-breaking study *Birds of America*, which was printed in four volumes between 1827 and 1838. This design was manufactured in more than one colourway, including a green and white combination on black ground. It would have been printed with an engraved metal roller created by a skilled draughtsman.

C88 M58 Y8 K1

C72 M45 Y87 K41

C37 M58 Y87 K25

C59 M67 Y25 K5

C33 M87 Y58 K22

C31 M42 Y91 K7

C26 M73 Y98 K16

Furnishing fabric 1837

Unknown artist/maker
Roller-printed cotton
UK

CIRC.370-1956
Given by the Calico Printers' Association

This early roller-printed fabric displays signs of the lack of precision that led some to associate this mass-printing method with a significant loss of quality. Flashes of undyed cotton are visible, and the areas of printed colour overlap the lines of the design to varying degrees. This means that the repeat pattern never quite repeats precisely. Although they would probably have been seen as defects at the time of manufacture, the fabric arguably derives a lively, relaxed style from such irregularities.

C20 M18 Y32 K0	
C67 M32 Y32 K2	C20 M97 Y90 K10
C26 M39 Y66 K2	C38 M24 Y29 K0	C37 M44 Y40 K3	C52 M75 Y64 K65

Furnishing fabric
c.1838

Unknown artist/maker

Block-printed cotton

UK

CIRC.610-1956
Given by Mrs Noah M. Eastwood

Floral textile motifs, long popular, received fresh impetus in the 1830s as technical improvements in printing combined with advances in dye chemistry meant that flowers could be reproduced with greater precision and detail. Increasingly elaborate floral designs were created for fashionable furnishing fabrics, like this piece, and also for women's dress fabrics, particularly day wear. Designers drew inspiration from nature as well as from botanical engravings and pattern books.

C82 M41 Y29 K3

C33 M46 Y78 K10

C16 M89 Y100 K6

C65 M32 Y96 K16

C18 M69 Y84 K4

C17 M22 Y85 K0

C40 M54 Y49 K10

C58 M74 Y70 K79

Cover
1840–70

Unknown artist/maker
Silk satin embroidered with
couched metal thread and silk
Iran

CIRC.157-1929
Given by J.B. Clarke-Thornhill

Small, usually square, embroidered covers like this one were used in Iran to wrap gifts and valued objects. They often incorporated silver and silver-gilt thread, made by wrapping thinly beaten silver wires around a silk thread. This not only created beautiful, luxurious pieces, but was also a form of portable wealth since such textiles could, if necessary, be burned and the metal salvaged. The silver threads are secured to the surface with tiny stitches in silk: a technique called couching. The pattern of flowers, leaves and meandering stems centres on a blossom with sixteen petals.

C80 M73 Y47 K40

C4 M18 Y66 K0

C34 M62 Y94 K24

C49 M68 Y81 K62

C8 M60 Y93 K1

C0 M3 Y22 K0

Fukusa
1840–70

Unknown artist/maker

Silk satin embroidered with silk and metallic thread

Japan

T.20-1923
Given by Mrs Watts

This textile cover is called a fukusa. Traditionally in Japan, gifts were placed in a box on a tray, over which a fukusa was draped. The choice of a fukusa appropriate to the occasion was an important part of the gift-giving ritual. The richness of the decoration was an indication of the donor's wealth, and the quality of the design evidence of his or her taste and sensibility. This satin fukusa is embroidered in silk and metallic thread with depictions of cranes. These birds are a symbol of longevity, once believed to live for a thousand years.

C30 M47 Y62 K5

C46 M74 Y59 K39

C21 M97 Y83 K12

C66 M38 Y96 K25

C53 M33 Y51 K5

C100 M83 Y15 K3

C50 M55 Y35 K7

C21 M18 Y43 K0

Design drawing
*c.*1848

A.W.N. Pugin (1812–52)
Brown, red, green, blue and white
bodycolour
UK

D.925-1908
Presented by J.D. Crace

The influential British architect and designer A.W.N. Pugin was known for his fiercely individual stylistic principles and, unusually, he worked alone on designs for every detail of his buildings. This design is probably for a carpet and was preserved by J.G. Crace, who ran an interior decorating firm that produced furniture, textiles and wallpapers to Pugin's designs. Pugin habitually used large-scale patterns in the Gothic style and drew on an extensive repertory of authentic details, based on his study of historical interiors. His work and writings inspired and shaped the Gothic Revival in Britain.

C72 M61 Y71 K74

C14 M29 Y58 K0

C56 M60 Y61 K36

C23 M23 Y52 K0

C22 M52 Y72 K4

C5 M11 Y23 K0

Fukusa
1850–67

Unknown artist/maker

Velvet embroidered with coloured
silk and gold-wrapped thread

Japan

701-1868

This example of a Japanese fukusa or
gift cover is embroidered in dazzling gold
thread, consisting of a silk core wrapped
in paper and gold leaf, on a black velvet
ground. It depicts the legend of Jo and
Uba, an old and happily married couple
whose spirits inhabit pine trees on the
shore of Lake Takasago. During the late
Victorian period in Britain it was very
fashionable to decorate the home with
Japanese textiles, which were considered
exotic and luxurious.

C35 M11 Y34 K0

C32 M49 Y59 K7

C16 M97 Y72 K4

C80 M43 Y77 K38

C2 M74 Y37 K0

C17 M35 Y100 K1

C66 M42 Y26 K2

C77 M80 Y55 K73

Furnishing fabric 1860–75

Unknown artist/maker

Printed cotton, glazed

France

T.424-1967
Given anonymously

The colours on this glazed-cotton French furnishing fabric are overprinted to obtain subtle shades of orange, brown, green and mauve. Among the birds depicted are a parrot with a green back, a cockatoo with a pink crest and breast, a bird of paradise and several hummingbirds.

C14 M22 Y35 K0

C77 M69 Y32 K77

C13 M99 Y100 K3

C63 M46 Y61 K24

C16 M30 Y83 K0

C87 M71 Y49 K45

Quilt
1864–77

Francis Brayley (d.1880)
Pieced wool, lined with damask
India

T.58-2007

Military or soldiers' quilts were sewn by soldiers from the wool serge or worsted twill used in military uniforms. This beautiful and brightly coloured example, made by a British soldier in India, has a complex geometric pattern of small hexagons forming six-pointed stars, large diamonds and hexagons in black, white, red, green and yellow. Piercing and sewing the thick cloth would have been an extremely difficult and time-consuming task. The quilt was made by Francis Brayley, a private in the 1st and 11th Regiment of Foot who served in India between 1864 and 1877 and died shortly after returning to Britain.

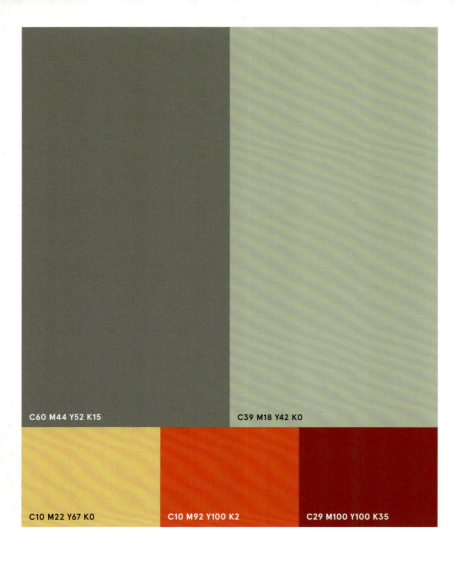

C60 M44 Y52 K15

C39 M18 Y42 K0

C10 M22 Y67 K0

C10 M92 Y100 K2

C29 M100 Y100 K35

Wallpaper
1872

Jeffrey & Co.
Colour woodblock print on paper
UK

E.1820-1934
Given by the Wallpaper Manufacturers Ltd

This elegantly balanced wallpaper design of redcurrants and foliage, by an unknown artist, was manufactured by Jeffrey & Co., a 19th-century British firm whose products regularly won medals and prizes for quality at international exhibitions. Jeffrey & Co. printed William Morris's wallpapers from 1864 onwards, and employed some of the best designers of the day, including Walter Crane, Lewis F. Day, B.J. Talbert and C.F.A. Voysey.

C11 M13 Y31 K0

C25 M23 Y52 K0

C13 M18 Y57 K0

C13 M51 Y51 K0

C21 M27 Y60 K0

C27 M51 Y60 K5

C25 M30 Y45 K0

The Sleeping Beauty Wallpaper 1879

Walter Crane (1845–1915) for Jeffrey & Co.
Colour machine print on paper
UK

E.60-1968
Given by Mrs Elisabet Hidemark

British artist and designer Walter Crane was also an illustrator of children's books, from which many of his illustrations were adapted as nursery wallpapers. Jeffrey & Co. produced this nursery paper as part of their range of Patent Hygienic Wallpapers. These were promoted as being free from arsenic (a toxic pigment often used in Victorian wallpapers) and washable. In 1880 Jeffrey & Co. re-issued the design, without the figures, as a block print called *The Briar Rose*.

C40 M28 Y21 K0

C64 M40 Y54 K14

C60 M49 Y53 K20

C26 M35 Y46 K1

C46 M71 Y68 K48

C20 M83 Y83 K9

C81 M69 Y25 K8

C31 M48 Y26 K0

C29 M38 Y70 K3

Wallpaper
c.1880–90

Unknown artist/maker
Colour machine print
UK

E.1822-1934
Given by the Wallpaper Manufacturers Ltd

This nursery wallpaper was probably manufactured by Heywood, Higginbottom & Smith, who patented a washable 'sanitary' wallpaper in 1871. The repeat pattern depicts fashionable men, women and children on bicycles and tricycles of a contemporary, albeit stylized, design. The development in the 1880s of 'safety bicycles' with two wheels of almost equal size encouraged more people to take up the new sport of cycling, although – as shown on this wallpaper design – falls and accidents could still happen.

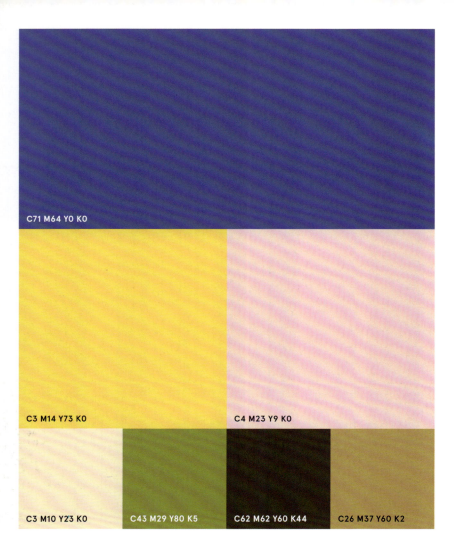

C71 M64 Y0 K0

C3 M14 Y73 K0

C4 M23 Y9 K0

C3 M10 Y23 K0

C43 M29 Y80 K5

C62 M62 Y60 K44

C26 M37 Y60 K2

Hindoo Gods
Wallpaper
1880–90

Allan, Cockshut & Co.
Colour machine print on paper
UK

E.1821-1934
Given by the Wallpaper Manufacturers Ltd

Europeans living in India in the 19th century found that the heat and humidity of the climate caused decorative papers to peel away from walls, so these wallpaper panels were probably used only as temporary decorations. The scene combines elements of European design (the chandeliers) with decorative features (the arch) characteristic of Indian art of the Mughal period (1526-1857). It depicts the Hindu god Vishnu, reclining on the celestial serpent Ananta Shesha, with the god Brahma appearing in a lotus flower growing from Vishnu's navel.

C13 M13 Y22 K1

C68 M38 Y28 K11

C20 M54 Y39 K7

C62 M42 Y84 K35

C29 M100 Y95 K35

C20 M40 Y90 K8

C45 M64 Y73 K66

C20 M58 Y90 K10

Lodden
Furnishing fabric
1883

William Morris (1834–96)
Block-printed cotton
UK

T.39-1919

After many years of experimentation, William Morris, designer, artist and entrepreneur, revived and perfected the process of indigo dyeing and discharge printing in 1881 when he established his own textile factory at Merton Abbey on the River Wandle. This pattern, *Lodden*, was designed to be discharge-printed leaving a white ground. The blue dye in this pattern is indigo. As a practical measure, Morris wore an indigo-dyed blue suit and shirt and used blue handkerchiefs when at work – similar in colour to the blue dye with which he was working.

C82 M50 Y49 K23

C0 M60 Y37 K0

C42 M27 Y51 K1

C3 M92 Y86 K0

C46 M67 Y70 K44

C12 M54 Y70 K1

C1 M11 Y7 K0

Cray
Furnishing fabric
1884

William Morris
Printed cotton
UK

T.613-1919

William Morris had a natural eye for pattern, and an ability to see designs as masses of shape and colour instead of series of lines. He trained his eye through extensive study of historical textiles and designs. This pattern, *Cray*, was one of a series of designs inspired by the diagonal lines in a piece of 17th-century Italian cut velvet seen by Morris at the V&A (V&A:442A-1883). Morris, equally inspired by the organic shapes of native British flowers, transformed the stiff lines of the original velvet into dynamic fabric designs.

C99 M88 Y30 K18

C26 M58 Y94 K10

C74 M34 Y45 K7

C8 M9 Y10 K0

Peacock Feathers
Furnishing fabric
1887

Arthur Silver (1853–96)
for Liberty & Co. Ltd

Roller-printed cotton

UK

T.50-1953
Given by Rex Silver, Esq.

The peacock feather, previously thought to be a symbol of bad luck, became an icon of the late 19th-century Aesthetic style. It was used in all forms of decoration and symbolized the movement's reputation for decadence. This furnishing fabric was printed relatively cheaply by roller. It proved popular and helped to establish Liberty & Co., founded in 1875, as one of the most fashionable shops and leading suppliers of artistic furnishings in London. Peacock feathers in their natural form were also often used in this period for fans and dress accessories, hung on walls and displayed in vases at home.

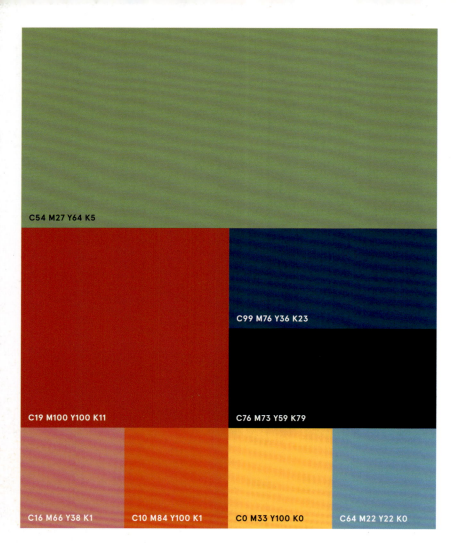

C54 M27 Y64 K5

C99 M76 Y36 K23

C19 M100 Y100 K11

C76 M73 Y59 K79

C16 M66 Y38 K1

C10 M84 Y100 K1

C0 M33 Y100 K0

C64 M22 Y22 K0

Detail of a suzani painting 1890

Unknown artist/maker

Opaque watercolour and gold on paper

India

IS.35-1992
Given by Mrs G.M. Hendley

A suzani is an embroidered cover or hanging, traditionally made from silk or cotton by women in Central Asia as a dowry piece. The name derives from the Persian for 'needle', and the practice of making suzanis is believed to have originated in Uzbekistan, Kyrgyzstan and Tajikistan and spread along the trading routes now termed the Silk Roads. This painting, made in Jaipur, India, is an intriguing record and celebration of the richly decorative detail of suzanis. It was most likely copied from an existing suzani by an art student studying design.

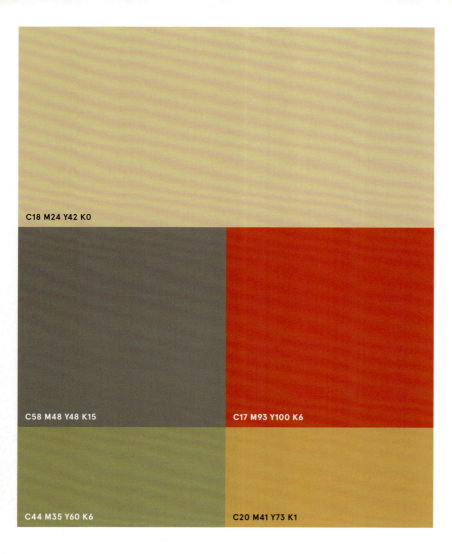

C18 M24 Y42 K0

C58 M48 Y48 K15

C17 M93 Y100 K6

C44 M35 Y60 K6

C20 M41 Y73 K1

Furnishing fabric
1890s

Sidney Mawson (1876–1937)
for Morton Sundour Fabric Ltd

Printed linen

UK

CIRC.97-1937
Given by the designer

Sidney Mawson was a freelance textile and wallpaper designer who had considerable success producing finely drawn naturalistic patterns in clear, bright colours, such as this furnishing fabric. The family-run company Morton Sundour Fabric Ltd was known for seeking out and commissioning work from the best British designers of the time, including C.F.A. Voysey and Lindsay Butterfield. This tradition is still sustained by Edinburgh Weavers, which was set up as an experimental branch of the company by Alastair Morton in 1928.

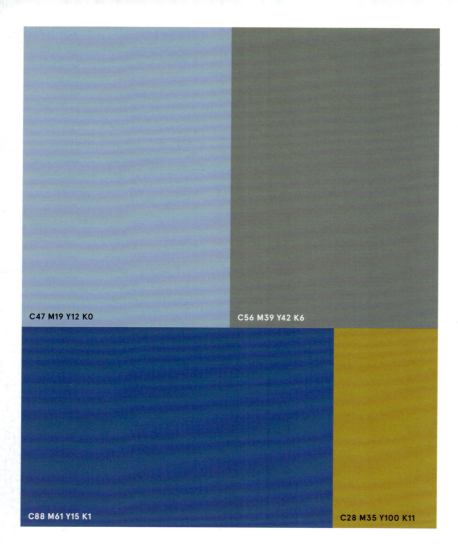

C47 M19 Y12 K0

C56 M39 Y42 K6

C88 M61 Y15 K1

C28 M35 Y100 K11

Sea Gulls
Design for a textile
1892

C.F.A. Voysey (1857–1941)
Pencil and watercolour
UK

E.147-1974

C.F.A. Voysey, one of the most influential pattern designers of his generation, began to design wallpapers, woven and printed textiles and carpets in the late 1880s. Bird motifs, as introduced in *Sea Gulls*, became a keynote of his work. In an interview in 1893 for *The Studio*, an illustrated fine arts and decorative arts magazine, Voysey remarked that the motifs on ornamental papers should not be restricted to foliage: 'I do not see why the forms of birds, for instance, may not be used provided they are reduced to mere symbols'.

C52 M33 Y48 K4

C98 M91 Y41 K42

C19 M26 Y54 K0

C27 M55 Y99 K11

C75 M47 Y70 K40

C17 M15 Y16 K0

Furnishing fabric 1897

The Silver Studio
for Liberty & Co. Ltd
Hand block-printed silk
UK

CIRC.233-1966
Given by Miss Mary Peerless

The Silver Studio, founded by designer Arthur Silver in 1880, was well known for its Art Nouveau designs and developed several commercially successful fabrics in this style for Liberty & Co. The Art Nouveau movement grew rapidly in the 1890s and by 1900 had spread across Europe to the USA and Russia, becoming the first international decorative style of the modern age. Its most characteristic form was the 'whiplash' line, a decorative line that writhes and coils with dynamic force. It can be seen here in the swirling leaves of this furnishing fabric.

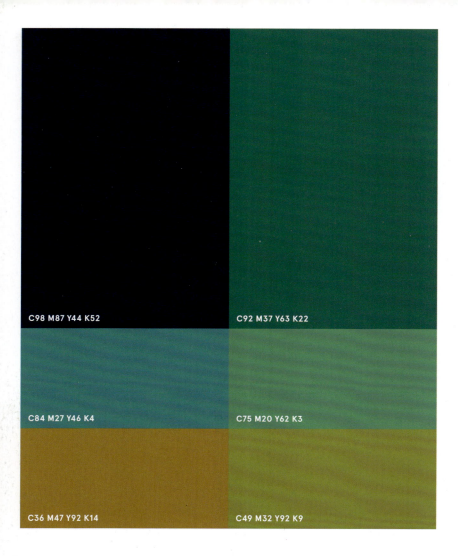

C98 M87 Y44 K52

C92 M37 Y63 K22

C84 M27 Y46 K4

C75 M20 Y62 K3

C36 M47 Y92 K14

C49 M32 Y92 K9

The Day Lily
Wallpaper
1897–8

Walter Crane for Jeffrey & Co.
Colour woodblock print on paper
UK

E.5149-1919

Walter Crane was a painter and illustrator, and also a designer of stained glass, metalwork, tiles, pottery, wallpapers and textiles. He produced many wallpaper designs; most of them were manufactured by Jeffrey & Co. This pattern of turquoise lilies on a dark blue background with large circles composed of small gold rings is ideal for block-printing, perhaps reflecting Crane's early apprenticeship to a wood-engraver.

C7 M13 Y29 K0

C64 M41 Y83 K27

C11 M45 Y93 K0

C27 M36 Y51 K1

C11 M75 Y73 K1

C52 M60 Y73 K46

C24 M59 Y98 K9

Cockatoo and Pomegranate
Wallpaper
1899

Walter Crane
Colour woodblock print on paper
UK

E.1761–1914
Given by Jeffrey & Co.

Jeffrey & Co. first commissioned Walter Crane to produce nursery wallpapers, based on his reputation as an illustrator of children's stories, and his later designs for other rooms in the house continued, with increasingly subtlety, to incorporate motifs inspired by myth, literature and fantasy. This design combines the rich symbolism of the pomegranate, which signifies fertility and abundance in many traditions, with that of the white cockatoo, often associated with spiritual transformation. This design was also produced on a light blue ground.

C87 M72 Y39 K26

C62 M43 Y31 K4

C26 M26 Y29 K0

C27 M47 Y44 K1

C47 M43 Y44 K6

Futon cover
Late 19th century

Unknown artist/maker
Resist-dyed cotton
Japan

T.199-1964

The design on this bedding (futon) cover has been created using a resist-dyeing technique called *tsutsugaki*, or 'tube drawing', in which a design is drawn on undyed cloth with paste made of rice flour, lime and water squeezed from a paper tube (*tsutsu*). The paste prevents the colour penetrating when the cloth is dyed. Once the dyed cloth is dry the paste is washed off and the process is repeated for various shades of blue; other colours are brushed on at the end. The pattern features roundels called *takara* ('precious designs') containing floral motifs, fish, cranes, tiger-cats, abstract medallions and symbols of money, in blue, grey and pink.

20th–21st century

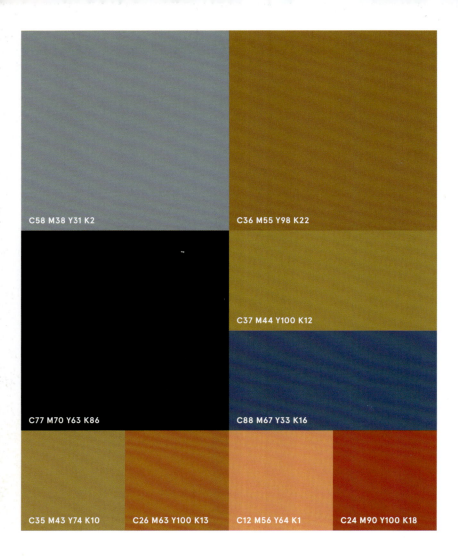

C58 M38 Y31 K2

C36 M55 Y98 K22

C37 M44 Y100 K12

C77 M70 Y63 K86

C88 M67 Y33 K16

C35 M43 Y74 K10

C26 M63 Y100 K13

C12 M56 Y64 K1

C24 M90 Y100 K18

Fukusa
20th century

Unknown artist/maker

Woven silk (*kesi*) with silk and golden-gilt threads

Japan

T.96-1967
Given by the Right Honourable
Viscount Bearsted

This large fukusa, or gift cover, depicts a legendary incident from the childhood of Chinese historian Sima Guang, known in Japanese as Shiba Onko. Sima Guang was playing with a group of friends when one of them fell into a large jar of water. The other children ran to get help, but quick-thinking Sima Guang broke the jar with a rock, saving his friend's life. All parts of the design are woven, with detailed features such as noses and ears skilfully delineated with slits, and outlines woven in contrasting tones or colours. Variations in colour are emphasized in places by use of thicker silk and a looser weave.

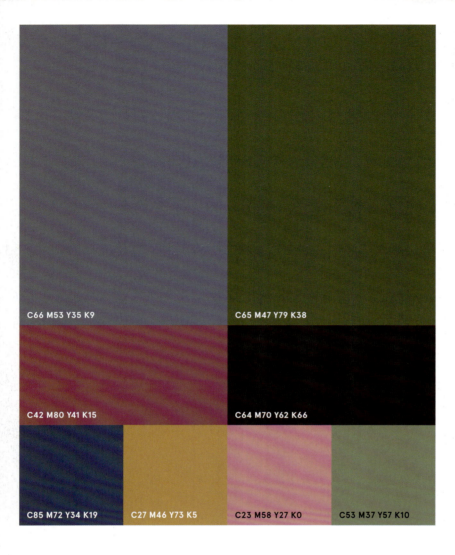

C66 M53 Y35 K9

C65 M47 Y79 K38

C42 M80 Y41 K15

C64 M70 Y62 K66

C85 M72 Y34 K19

C27 M46 Y73 K5

C23 M58 Y27 K0

C53 M37 Y57 K10

Thistle
Furnishing fabric
*c.*1900

Harry Napper (1860–1930)
for Liberty & Co. Ltd

Block-printed linen and cotton

UK

T.53-1953
Given by G. P. & J. Baker Ltd.

This printed cotton furnishing fabric was designed by Harry Napper, one of the most successful commercial designers of the late Victorian period. Absorbing the most fashionable elements of British and Continental design at the end of the 19th century, Napper produced a range of very popular stylized floral designs, such as this one. He sold to many manufacturers, including G. P. & J. Baker and his textiles were particularly popular in France.

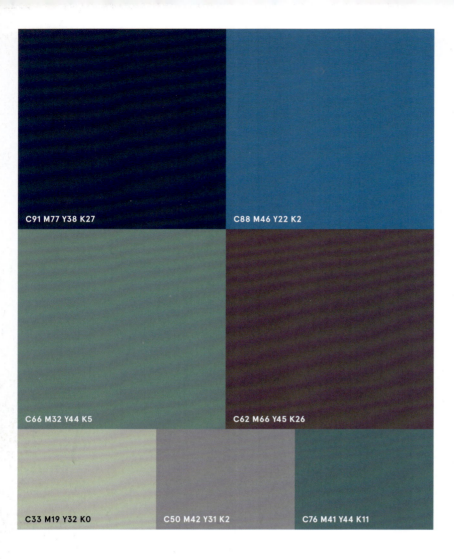

C91 M77 Y38 K27

C88 M46 Y22 K2

C66 M32 Y44 K5

C62 M66 Y45 K26

C33 M19 Y32 K0

C50 M42 Y31 K2

C76 M41 Y44 K11

Columbine
Wallpaper
1901

Allan Vigers (1858–1921)
for Jeffrey & Co.

Colour woodblock print on paper
UK

E.2369-1932
Given by Harris & Sons

Like several other Arts and Crafts textile designers, including C.F.A. Voysey and William Morris, Allan Vigers trained as an architect before moving into the applied arts. This architectural sensibility is reflected in the balanced yet dynamic structures of many Arts and Crafts wallpaper and textile patterns, in which the organic, luxuriant natural forms of plants and flowers are elegantly contained within carefully constructed repeat patterns.

C66 M56 Y50 K26

C42 M40 Y79 K12

C73 M49 Y71 K65

C27 M30 Y55 K1

C34 M55 Y62 K11

C22 M30 Y83 K1

C26 M62 Y79 K10

C20 M88 Y91 K9

The River Rug
1903

C.F.A. Voysey

Hand-knotted in wool on a canvas
base with a cotton warp and
probably linen weft

UK

T.71-2014
Accepted in lieu of Inheritance Tax
by HM Government and allocated to
the Victoria and Albert Museum, 2014

The River Rug was probably intended as
a hearth rug, perhaps for C.F.A. Voysey's
own family home. Its very unusual design
may have been planned with Voysey's own
children in mind, as its many fascinating
details include a miniature version of
Voysey's family home, The Orchard.
The rug stands out among Voysey's other
textiles, which feature stylized, regular
arrangements of animal and plant forms.
It may have been inspired by the
16th-century Sheldon tapestry maps of
English counties, although when it was
exhibited at the Arts and Crafts Exhibition
Society in 1903, it was thought to be
reminiscent of Chinese textiles.

C45 M17 Y38 K0

C20 M6 Y20 K0

C53 M21 Y61 K2

C14 M26 Y66 K0

C24 M53 Y85 K6

C11 M5 Y16 K0

C12 M15 Y14 K0

Furnishing fabric 1903

Steiner & Co.
Printed cotton
UK

T.171-1957

Textile printers Steiner & Co., founded in Lancashire in the 1840s by chemist Frederick Steiner, were enthusiastic proponents of Art Nouveau style displayed in the scrolling floral pattern of this fabric. They produced several fabrics in astringent colours and sourced designs from France and Belgium as well as from British studios familiar with the Continental market, such as the Silver Studio. Steiner & Co. were one of the few Lancashire printers to remain independent of the Calico Printers' Association, a combine that controlled over half of Britain's textile printing industry at the start of the 20th century.

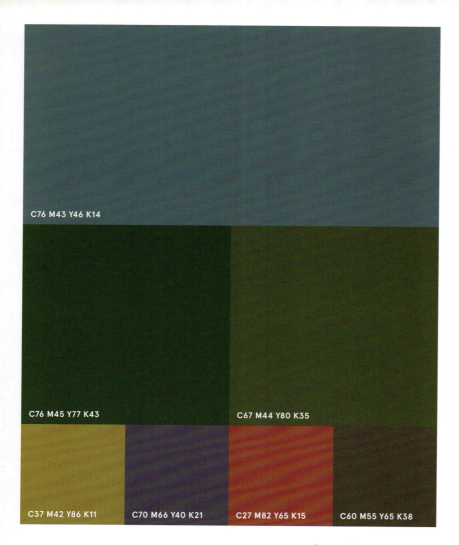

C76 M43 Y46 K14

C76 M45 Y77 K43

C67 M44 Y80 K35

C37 M42 Y86 K11

C70 M66 Y40 K21

C27 M82 Y65 K15

C60 M55 Y65 K38

Macaw
Wallpaper
1908

Walter Crane for Jeffrey & Co.
Colour woodblock print on paper
UK

E.1763-1914
Given by Jeffrey & Co.

Influenced by William Morris and
the Socialist movement, Walter Crane
developed a range of wallpapers and
furnishing textiles from the early 1880s
in order to bring art into the daily lives
of the general public. In this example,
his experience as an illustrator of
children's books is clearly revealed.
This dramatic design with a large repeat
is typical of Crane's later wallpapers,
which feature dense foliage with fruit
(here orange trees and grape vines)
and exotic birds.

C14 M17 Y24 K0

C30 M25 Y56 K1

C58 M44 Y53 K15

C42 M30 Y38 K0

C14 M34 Y64 K0

Design for a printed textile *c.*1910

Lindsay Phillip Butterfield
(1869–1948)

Painting, watercolour
and bodycolour on paper

UK

E.3044-1934
Given by the artist

Lindsay Butterfield, like several of his contemporaries in the growing field of textile design, was first apprenticed to an architect before developing his career in the applied arts. He studied pattern design at the National Art Training School (now the Royal College of Art) and would have become familiar with the study collections of the V&A at this time. He admired C.F.A. Voysey and William Morris, and his work shows their influence while also possessing its own fresh and unforced aesthetic. His designs have been seen as a bridge between the Arts and Crafts movement and the looser, flowing styles associated with Art Nouveau.

C28 M46 Y83 K6	C79 M64 Y52 K43
C21 M67 Y78 K5	C62 M55 Y15 K1
C18 M33 Y27 K0	C60 M66 Y48 K29

Design for a tapestry 1911

Kathleen Kersey (b.1899)
Pencil, watercolour and bodycolour, mounted on thick card
UK

E.690-1993

This design was entered by Kathleen Kersey as a student work for the National Art Competition in 1911. It is lettered in ink with her name and age, '22'. The placement of exotic monkeys alongside more commonplace squirrels, blackberries and forget-me-nots in an elaborate pattern of foliage is unusual. The complexity of the pattern is cleverly masked by its harmonious colour scheme. Kersey created the still-popular wallpaper design *Arbutus* for Morris & Co. shortly afterwards, in 1913.

C23 M26 Y40 K0

C80 M65 Y33 K15

C23 M84 Y82 K13

C54 M72 Y42 K21

C35 M89 Y83 K52

C22 M79 Y100 K12

Margery Textile 1913

Roger Fry (1866–1934)
for Omega Workshops

Block-printed linen

UK/France

T.386-1913
Given by Roger Fry

The Omega Workshops were founded in 1913 by painter, art critic and Bloomsbury Group member Roger Fry, who brought together artists to design furniture, pottery, glass, textiles and entire schemes of interior decoration. Their radically abstract style, typified by this textile, was influenced by developments in contemporary painting. In keeping with the painting tradition, Fry believed that designs should not be too mechanical and should show evidence of the artist's hand. The workshops produced six printed linens, which were used by the most daring clients as dress fabrics. *Margery* was named for one of Fry's five sisters.

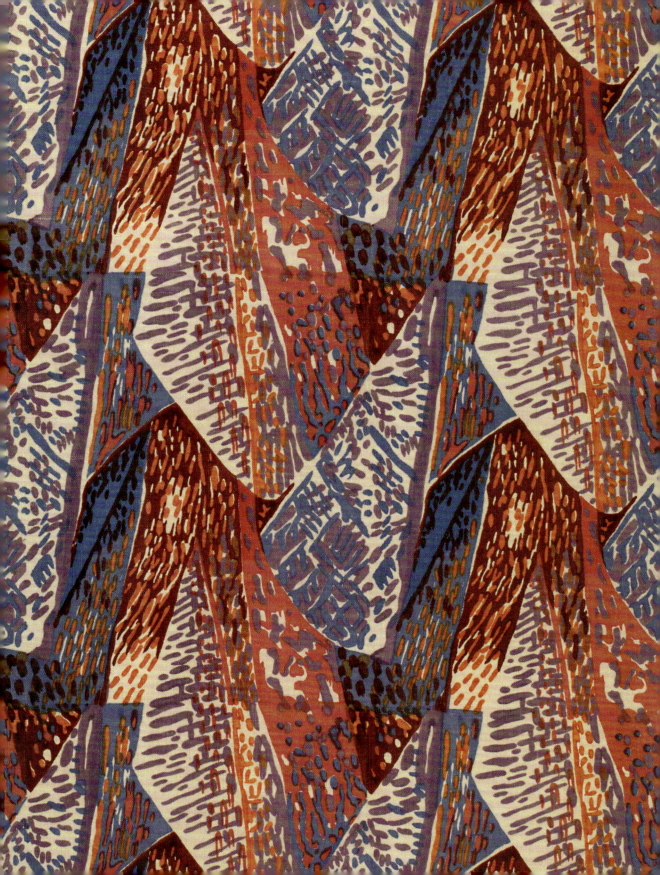

C17 M79 Y100 K6

C55 M33 Y54 K6

C100 M84 Y35 K23

C60 M68 Y69 K71

C17 M15 Y22 K0

Maud
Textile
*c.*1913

Vanessa Bell (1879–1961)
for Omega Workshops

Printed linen

UK/France

T.388-1913
Given by Roger Fry

This striking fabric was designed for the Omega Workshops by Vanessa Bell, a pioneering Bloomsbury Group artist whose practice moved freely between fine and applied art. The design was probably named after Lady Maud Cunard, a bohemian society figure. It is an early example of the application of abstract art to a British textile and was described upon its acquisition by the V&A in 1913 as a 'specimen of "post-impressionism" as applied to the printing of linen fabrics'. Similar bold black lines and blocks of colour are found in a few other Omega designs, anticipating the jazzy Art Deco textiles of the 1920s and '30s.

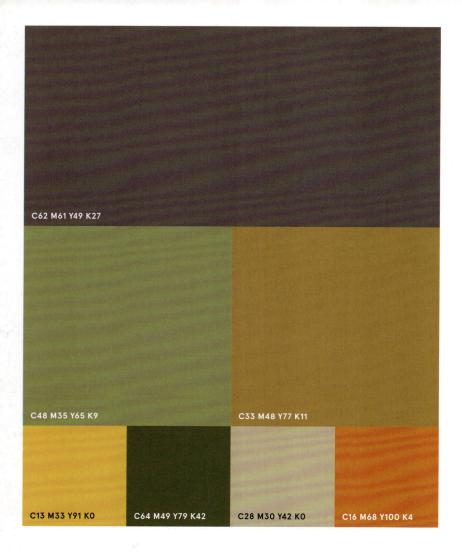

C62 M61 Y49 K27

C48 M35 Y65 K9

C33 M48 Y77 K11

C13 M33 Y91 K0

C64 M49 Y79 K42

C28 M30 Y42 K0

C16 M68 Y100 K4

Furnishing fabric
*c.*1914

C.F.A. Voysey for Morton Sundour
Fabric Ltd

Printed cotton

UK

T.31-1953
Given by C. Cowles Voysey, FRIBA

C.F.A. Voysey, like William Morris, advocated studying and taking direct inspiration from the natural world. He incorporated birds, plant forms and animal motifs into the majority of his designs, developing fresh and original combinations with remarkable inventiveness over his prolific career, which lasted five decades. His work forms a vital link between the Arts and Crafts movement and Modernism and was extremely influential in both Britain and Europe. This furnishing fabric featuring wildflowers, blackberries and birds was part of a series for Morton Sundour entitled *Cumberland Prints*.

C10 M8 Y14 K0

C34 M11 Y31 K0

C24 M38 Y100 K2

C5 M43 Y99 K0

C88 M76 Y33 K19

Design for a textile 1918

C.F.A. Voysey
Watercolour and pencil on paper
UK

E.217-1974
Given by Courtaulds Ltd

The small dark blue area in the top left of this design for a pattern featuring lions, palm fronds and flowers shows Voysey experimenting with different colourways and is accompanied by a pencil note: 'alternative treatment'. It is signed 'C.F.A. Voysey, Archt.' An architect as well as a designer, Voysey was often involved in every aspect of the interior design of a house, from wallpaper and curtains to furniture.

C14 M17 Y12 K0

C60 M69 Y67 K70

C38 M55 Y91 K23

C59 M65 Y46 K25

C66 M52 Y65 K37

C77 M75 Y39 K27

Furnishing fabric 1918

Charles Rennie Mackintosh (1868–1928) for William Foxton Ltd

Printed cotton

UK

T.85-1979
Given by Manchester Design Registry

Charles Rennie Mackintosh designed this textile in 1918. The purple and green colours are typical of the bright tones of the era. Mackintosh was ahead of his time in experimenting with geometrization and the flattening of forms. These were features that later became characteristic of Art Deco. From 1915 to 1923 Mackintosh lived in London, where he was unable to attract commissions as an architect. He created textiles for William Foxton Ltd, the most innovative furnishing textile firm in Britain during this period.

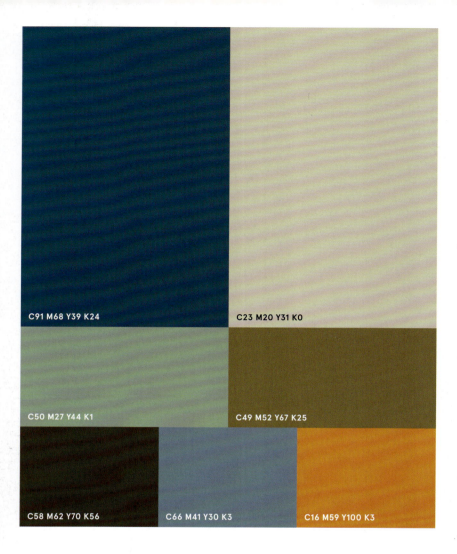

C91 M68 Y39 K24

C23 M20 Y31 K0

C50 M27 Y44 K1

C49 M52 Y67 K25

C58 M62 Y70 K56

C66 M41 Y30 K3

C16 M59 Y100 K3

Furnishing fabric
c.1918

Constance Irving (fl.1911–29)
for William Foxton Ltd

Roller-printed cotton

UK

CIRC.624-1956
Given by Miss Minnie McLeish

Constance Irving was among the innovative British artists (including Augustus John, John Lavery, Philip Wilson Steer and Henry Tonks) who exhibited work in the second Post-Impressionist and Cubist exhibition in Liverpool in 1911, which was only the second time that works by Gauguin, Van Gogh, Cézanne, Matisse and Picasso were shown in the UK. Irving supplied a number of designs for William Foxton Ltd during the 1920s; her painterly style embraced both colourful florals and bold, abstract patterns. Both aspects are reflected in this fabric design of geometric circles with abstracted flowers and leaves.

C40 M53 Y70 K19

C4 M17 Y40 K0

C2 M19 Y84 K0

C31 M79 Y75 K27

C65 M64 Y65 K61

C62 M25 Y52 K3

Design for a carpet 1919–29

Eileen Gray (1878–1976)
Gouache on paper
France

CIRC.239-1973

Irish architect and designer Eileen Gray trained at the Slade School of Fine Art in London and settled in Paris in 1907. This carpet design, created in gouache on rough-textured paper, was probably made for her Paris gallery, Galerie Jean Désert. Gray's first architectural work, E1027 on the Côte d'Azur, built in 1929, is now recognized as an iconic Modernist building. In addition to the house itself, Gray designed all its furniture and furnishings.

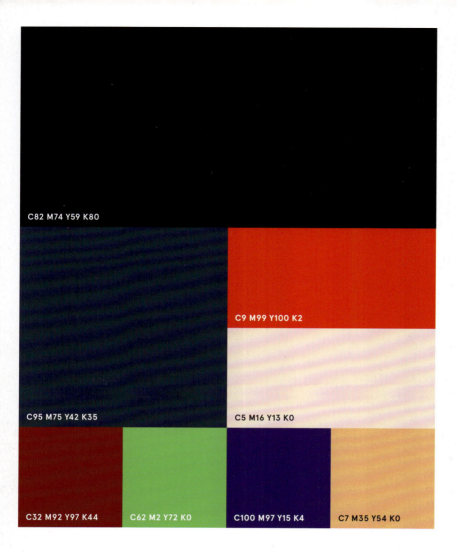

C82 M74 Y59 K80

C9 M99 Y100 K2

C95 M75 Y42 K35

C5 M16 Y13 K0

C32 M92 Y97 K44

C62 M2 Y72 K0

C100 M97 Y15 K4

C7 M35 Y54 K0

Quilt cover
1920–40

Unknown artist/maker

Plain-weave cotton with stencil
resist-dyed decoration

China

FE.19-1984

This is a cotton wedding quilt cover from
the Republican period in China (1911–49).
It was made in Fujian Province, perhaps
by a Fujianese craftsman or woman who
had gone to learn the technical skills
of batik in Java and then returned home.
It represents one of a number of Chinese
craft initiatives during the 1920s and
'30s that mid-century political turmoil
prevented from coming to the notice
of the wider world at the time.

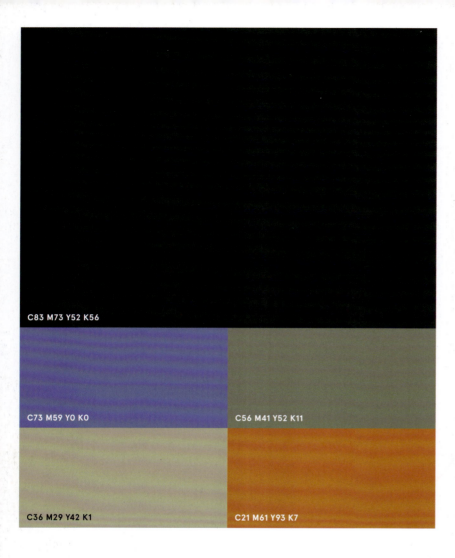

C83 M73 Y52 K56

C73 M59 Y0 K0

C56 M41 Y52 K11

C36 M29 Y42 K1

C21 M61 Y93 K7

Furnishing fabric 1921

Constance Irving
for William Foxton Ltd
Roller-printed cotton
UK

CIRC.621-1956
Given by Miss Minnie McLeish

William Foxton Ltd produced some of the most interesting artist-designed printed furnishings of the 1920s. The firm's founder, William Foxton, was an early member of the Design and Industries Association (DIA), formed in 1915 with the specific remit to raise the standard of British design. Foxton subsequently commissioned designs from innovative artists and designers, including Constance Irving and Charles Rennie Mackintosh. This striking pattern by Irving, a design of abstract stems, flowers and looping tendrils in blue, sage green and rust on a black background, was extremely modern and forward-looking for its time.

C23 M41 Y84 K2

C69 M67 Y34 K15

C31 M64 Y100 K21

C16 M19 Y23 K0

C65 M39 Y39 K6

Furnishing fabric 1922

Charles Rennie Mackintosh for William Foxton Ltd

Roller-printed cretonne

UK

T.439-1934
Given by the British Institute of Industrial Arts

This textile was designed by Charles Rennie Mackintosh for William Foxton Ltd in 1922. The pattern mimics the compartmentalized areas filled with small-scale decoration found in Indonesian batik designs. The craft of batik came to Europe from Indonesia via the Netherlands. It was popularized during the 1920s by practitioners such as Mme Pangon in Paris and Jessie M. King of the Glasgow School of Art. The technique involves applying wax to the textile to protect the patterned areas before placing it in a dye bath. The process can then be repeated by removing areas of wax and dyeing the exposed parts with further colours.

20TH–21ST CENTURY

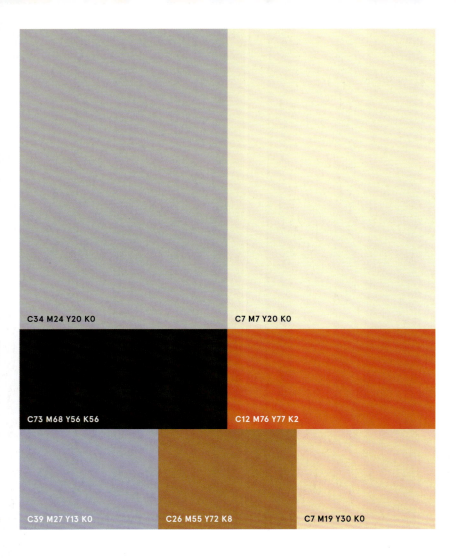

C34 M24 Y20 K0

C7 M7 Y20 K0

C73 M68 Y56 K56

C12 M76 Y77 K2

C39 M27 Y13 K0

C26 M55 Y72 K8

C7 M19 Y30 K0

Design for a hanging 1927

Gunta Stölzl (1897–1983)
for the Bauhaus

Watercolour, pencil, ink
and gouache

Germany

CIRC.701-1967

Textile artist Gunta Stölzl played a
fundamental role in the development of
the Bauhaus School's weaving workshop,
becoming its first female master in 1925.
This design for a hanging was made in the
years following her formal appointment
as director of the workshop in 1926.
She had previously studied at the Bauhaus
with artists Johannes Itten and Paul Klee,
and brought her knowledge of fine art and
colour theory to bear on the creation of
highly original and beautiful woven textiles.

C25 M42 Y45 K1

C46 M50 Y51 K13

C20 M40 Y66 K1

C64 M33 Y61 K11

C83 M47 Y68 K41

C55 M48 Y38 K8

C19 M92 Y81 K8

C17 M62 Y50 K1

C42 M76 Y42 K14

C100 M92 Y23 K9

C38 M77 Y91 K51

Furnishing fabric 1928

Minnie McLeish (1876–1957)
for William Foxton Ltd

Roller-printed cotton

UK

T.400-1934
Given by the British Institute of
Industrial Arts

This furnishing fabric was designed
by Minnie McLeish in 1928. The boldly
coloured abstract, painterly flowers
show the influence of Cubism. McLeish
created a number of other floral, painterly
furnishing fabrics as a freelance designer
for William Foxton Ltd, which also
commissioned artists such as Charles
Rennie Mackintosh, Claude Lovat Fraser,
F. Gregory Brown and Constance Irving.

C9 M8 Y12 K0

C8 M70 Y100 K1

C84 M78 Y0 K0

C49 M29 Y100 K7

C18 M31 Y100 K1

C80 M90 Y24 K11

C25 M45 Y98 K5

Aralia
Furnishing fabric
*c.*1930

Josef Frank (1885–1967)
for Haus & Garten

Block-printed linen

Austria

CIRC.823-1967
Given by J.W.F. Morton, Esq.

Aralia, a large and bold design for its time, was a furnishing fabric created for a house in the fashionable Hohe Warte district of Vienna. The large leaves in the print, by Austrian-born architect and designer Josef Frank, closely reproduce those of the potted aralia (or spikenard) plant. Frank founded the Haus & Garten interior firm in 1925 with architects Oskar Wlach and Walter Sobotka. Despite his status as a leading figure of early Viennese Modernism, Frank did not subscribe to puritanical, Minimalist design ideals, favouring instead idiosyncratic, colourful and non-uniform interior schemes.

C16 M13 Y30 K0

C2 M1 Y16 K0

C27 M24 Y44 K0

C43 M19 Y34 K11

C39 M39 Y56 K6

C28 M16 Y42 K0

Furnishing fabric
*c.*1930

Betty Joel Ltd
Silk and cotton damask
France

CIRC.26-1936
Given by Betty Joel Ltd

This damask furnishing fabric was woven
in France in about 1930 for Betty Joel Ltd.
It depicts stylized clouds, stormy weather
and rough seas, following the 1930s trend
for increasingly abstract designs in muted
colours. Joel (1894–1985) was a furniture
and interior designer who sold French
furnishings from the 1920s onwards from
her showroom in Sloane Street, London.

C8 M10 Y20 K0

C73 M42 Y73 K30

C29 M11 Y49 K0

C27 M74 Y91 K18

C0 M89 Y100 K0

Leaf
Wallpaper
*c.*1930

Edward Bawden (1903–89)
for Curwen Press Ltd
Colour lithograph on paper
UK

E.546-1931

Edward Bawden was a versatile and skilled artist whose practice successfully combined fine and commercial art. He was well known as a watercolour painter and printmaker. The delicate clarity of this wallpaper design demonstrates Bawden's sensitive and original use of colour and composition.

C5 M22 Y31 K0

C50 M31 Y72 K8

C56 M53 Y47 K17

C16 M35 Y68 K1

C17 M61 Y84 K3

C75 M76 Y57 K76

C17 M88 Y96 K6

Kruger National Park
Furnishing fabric 1930s

Edinburgh Weavers
Printed cotton
UK

T.151-2009
Given by Sara Lee Courtaulds

Edinburgh Weavers was founded in 1928 as an experimental design and marketing unit of Morton Sundour Fabrics Ltd and remains in operation today. The firm achieved success in the UK and USA under the enlightened directorship of Alastair Morton (1910–63), who commissioned freelance designers and artists to produce work for interpretation as printed and woven fabrics. This quirky design is inspired by the wildlife of Kruger National Park in north-eastern South Africa.

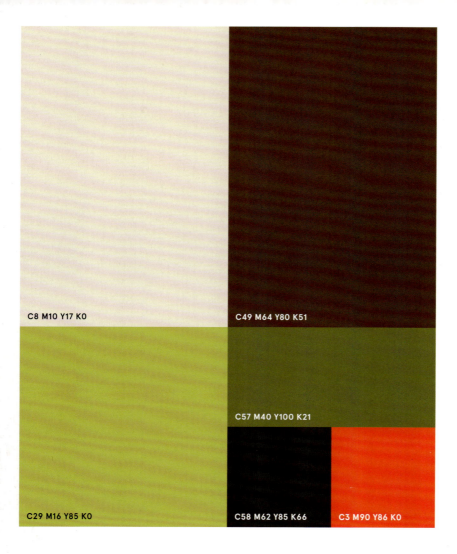

C8 M10 Y17 K0

C49 M64 Y80 K51

C29 M16 Y85 K0

C57 M40 Y100 K21

C58 M62 Y85 K66

C3 M90 Y86 K0

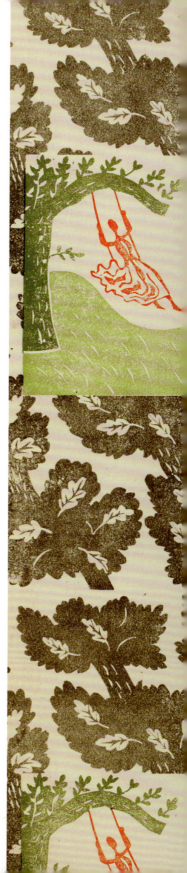

Knole Park
Wallpaper
c.1931

Edward Bawden
Colour hand-print in distemper
from lino blocks on paper
UK

E.960-1978

Edward Bawden began designing wallpapers in collaboration with the artist John Aldridge in the late 1920s. At first they painstakingly printed the papers themselves from lino blocks in a small attic studio at Bawden's Essex home; later the blocks were transferred to John Perry & Co. who produced the wallpapers from them. Knole Park, home to the aristocratic Sackville family since 1603, is a sprawling, atmospheric estate in Kent filled with oak trees and herds of deer, both referenced in this design.

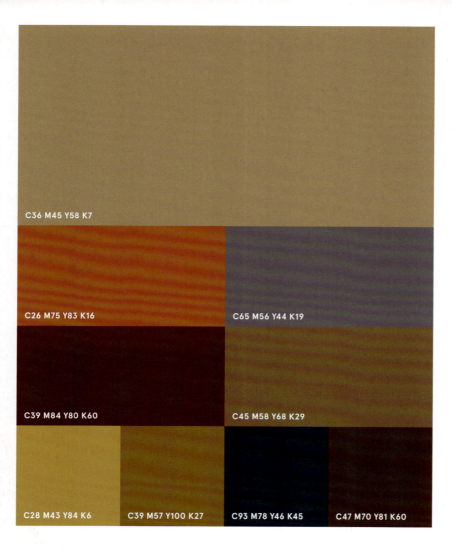

C36 M45 Y58 K7

C26 M75 Y83 K16

C65 M56 Y44 K19

C39 M84 Y80 K60

C45 M58 Y68 K29

C28 M43 Y84 K6

C39 M57 Y100 K27

C93 M78 Y46 K45

C47 M70 Y81 K60

Ayesha
Furnishing fabric
1931

Silver Studio for Liberty & Co. Ltd
Printed cotton
UK

T.14-1975
Given by Manchester Design Registry

This fabric design – featuring deer, birds and interlacing stems with leaves and blossoms – was printed in a variety of colourways, including a lighter pink, green and blue combination on a cream ground. It was designed by the Silver Studio, which, despite having fewer than fifteen staff members during the early 1930s, continued to be influential and created around 800 designs annually during this period. Several were mass-produced and sold across Europe, and consequently found their way into many homes.

C83 M72 Y56 K66

C52 M43 Y44 K8

C49 M27 Y59 K3

C28 M51 Y92 K9

C13 M69 Y80 K2

C18 M19 Y25 K0

C32 M22 Y64 K1

C28 M100 Y93 K34

Furnishing fabric 1932

Sidney Mawson for Arthur Sanderson & Sons Ltd

Block-printed linen

UK

CIRC.530-1966
Given by the Manchester Design Registry

This elegantly symmetrical furnishing fabric design by Sidney Mawson, based around the naturalistic curling shapes of stems and flower petals, shows the continued influence and popularity of the principles of pattern established by William Morris and the Arts and Crafts movement. Mawson, a successful freelance designer, worked for a range of clients including Liberty & Co. and Morton Sundour Fabrics Ltd, as well as Arthur Sanderson & Sons Ltd, founded in 1860.

C14 M13 Y26 K0

C42 M26 Y32 K0

C21 M30 Y40 K0

C24 M64 Y78 K10

C21 M42 Y31 K0

C17 M30 Y90 K1

Daphne and Apollo
Textile
1932

Duncan Grant (1885–1978)
for Allan Walton Textiles

Printed satin

UK

CIRC.357&C-1938

Artist and Bloomsbury Group member Duncan Grant collaborated with Vanessa Bell in the production of several interior schemes in the 1920s and '30s, many including rugs, printed furnishings and embroideries. His designs for printed textiles were produced by Allan Walton, textile designer, manufacturer and interior decorator. Walton commissioned some of the most enterprising artist-designed printed fabrics of the 1930s. This fabric is inspired by the ancient Greek myth of the god Apollo's passion for the nymph Daphne, who transformed herself into a laurel tree to escape his pursuit.

C18 M35 Y100 K1

C67 M67 Y64 K70

C22 M19 Y23 K0

C45 M39 Y44 K4

C35 M60 Y100 K24

Grapes
Furnishing fabric
1932

Duncan Grant for Allan Walton
Textiles

Printed linen

UK

CIRC.236-1935

Printed linen of this design – featuring
grey and white grapes, blossoms,
leaves and vines – was used for the
upholstery and drapery of a music room
collaboratively designed by Bloomsbury
Group artists Duncan Grant and Vanessa
Bell and displayed at the Lefevre Gallery
in London. *Grapes* can be seen today,
in a pink colourway, in the library of
Charleston, Bell's former home in Sussex.

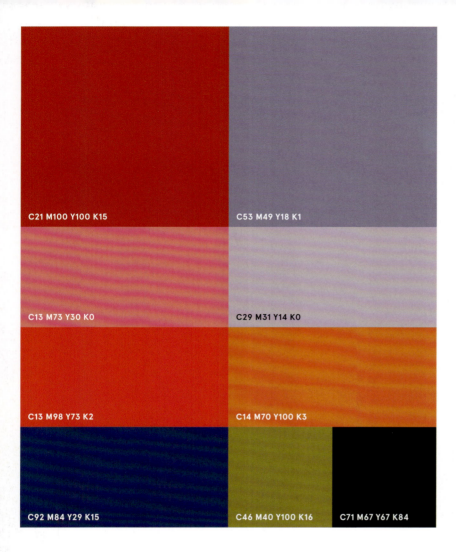

C21 M100 Y100 K15

C53 M49 Y18 K1

C13 M73 Y30 K0

C29 M31 Y14 K0

C13 M98 Y73 K2

C14 M70 Y100 K3

C92 M84 Y29 K15

C46 M40 Y100 K16

C71 M67 Y67 K84

Furnishing fabric 1933

Calico Printers' Association
Roller-printed cotton
UK

T.100-1979
Given by the Manchester Design Registry

The design of this fabric is of overlapping diamond shapes filled in with brushstrokes in bright colours. It resembles many French fabrics of the period, which were inspired by abstract art movements such as Cubism.

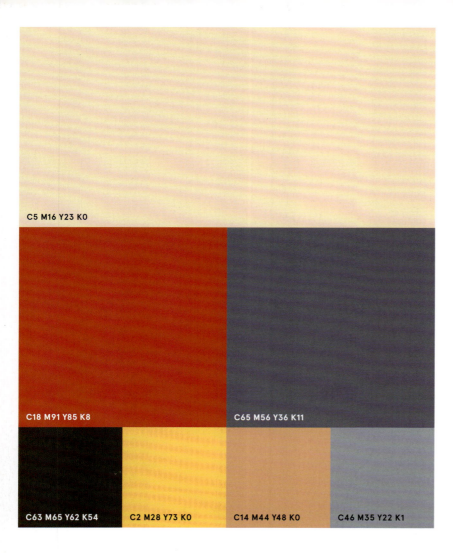

C5 M16 Y23 K0

C18 M91 Y85 K8

C65 M56 Y36 K11

C63 M65 Y62 K54

C2 M28 Y73 K0

C14 M44 Y48 K0

C46 M35 Y22 K1

Furnishing fabric
1933

Josef Hillerbrand (1892–1981)

Printed linen

UK

T.38:1, 2-2009
Given by Sara Lee Courtaulds

Alastair Morton, director of Edinburgh Weavers, met German designer Josef Hillerbrand during a visit to Munich in 1932. Two colourful and bold foliage patterns by Hillerbrand appeared in a collection of screen-printed textiles produced by Edinburgh Weavers the following year. Their bright colours were related to the vibrant style of the Wiener Werkstätte, but excitingly different from other textiles available in Britain at the time.

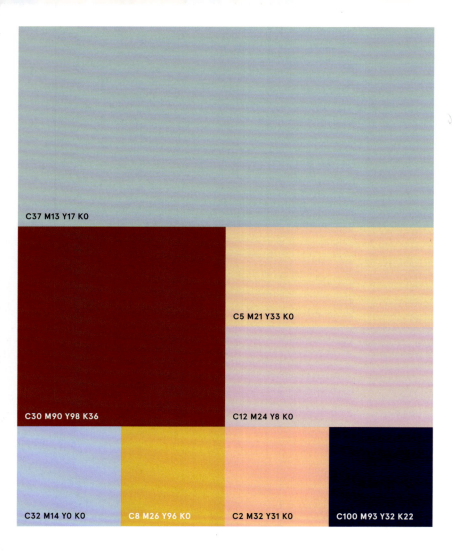

C37 M13 Y17 K0

C5 M21 Y33 K0

C30 M90 Y98 K36

C12 M24 Y8 K0

C32 M14 Y0 K0

C8 M26 Y96 K0

C2 M32 Y31 K0

C100 M93 Y32 K22

Queen Mary
Furnishing fabric
1935–6

Duncan Grant for
Allan Walton Textiles

Screen-printed cotton velvet

UK

CIRC.410-1954

This fabric was designed by Duncan Grant for use in the First Class Lounge of the RMS *Queen Mary*, the Cunard ocean liner built in 1934. Grant was commissioned in 1935 to create a complete interior for the lounge, including large-scale mural paintings and furnishings. His designs were unfortunately later rejected by the chairman and directors of Cunard; their original enthusiasm for commissioning a modern artist had waned. Although Grant's fee was paid, none of his work was used in the final decorative scheme.

C49 M34 Y45 K3

C31 M70 Y89 K24

C37 M25 Y37 K1

Grass and Swan
Wallpaper
1939

Edward Bawden

Colour hand-print in distemper
from lino blocks on paper

UK

E.1635-1939

This delicate design was hand-printed in
distemper from linoleum blocks designed
and cut by Edward Bawden himself.
It was marketed by Cole & Son as one of
'The Bardfield Wallpapers', named for the
Essex village to which Bawden and fellow
artist Eric Ravilious moved in 1931 and
where, over several decades, an artistic
community formed around them. Although
the design is dated 1939, its commercial
production was interrupted by the Second
World War and did not begin until 1946.
At that time, the wallpapers were
produced in limited quantities to order
and were relatively expensive.

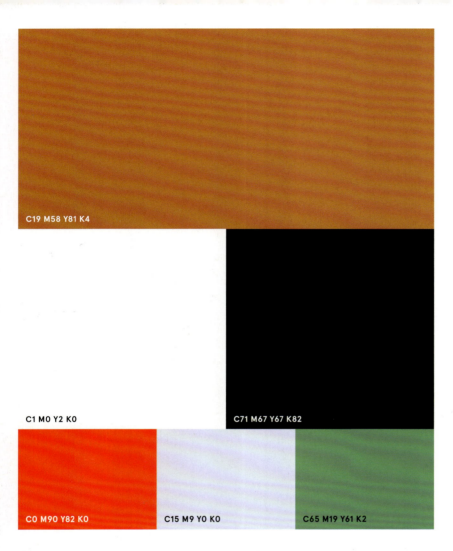

C19 M58 Y81 K4

C1 M0 Y2 K0

C71 M67 Y67 K82

C0 M90 Y82 K0

C15 M9 Y0 K0

C65 M19 Y61 K2

Spring Rain
**Furnishing fabric
1950s**

Salvador Dalí (1904–89)
for Schiffer Prints

Hand-printed with vat dyes

USA

CIRC.137-1950
Given by Schiffer Prints

Established by Milton Schiffer in 1945, Schiffer Prints was a division of the American firm Mil-Art Company Inc. To revitalize the company's fortunes after the war, Schiffer invited architects, designers and painters to create designs for printed fabrics. One such design, by famed Surrealist artist Salvador Dalí, was *Spring Rain*, with its vividly coloured geometric raindrops. Dalí also designed fabrics for Welsey Simpson (1944), curtains and drapes for Sterling (1949), rugs for Mohawk (1952) and ties for McCurach (1944).

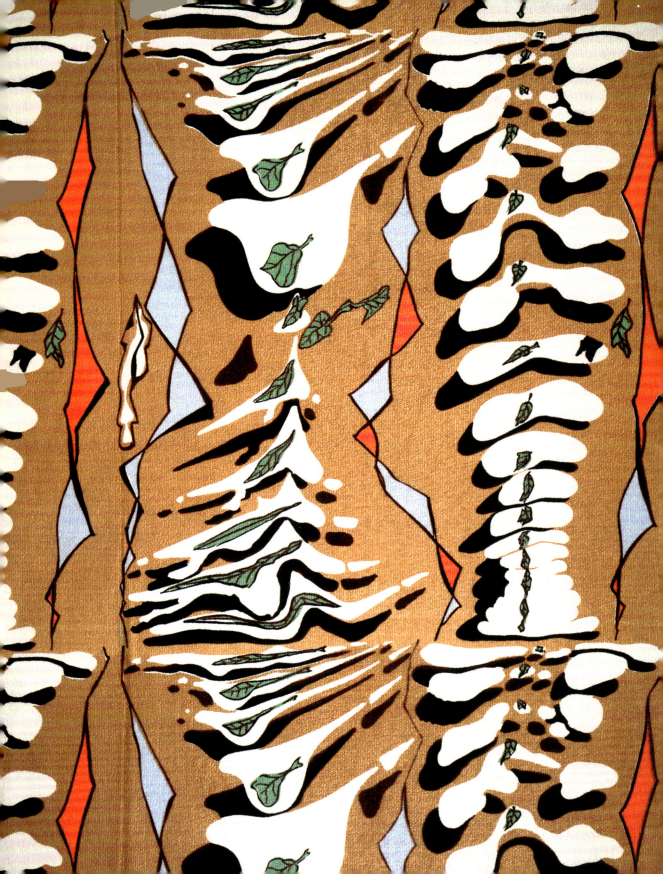

C62 M49 Y79 K40	C74 M0 Y48 K0
C31 M21 Y63 K1	C22 M43 Y100 K3
C78 M49 Y75 K51	C77 M61 Y68 K72
	C9 M0 Y73 K0
	C3 M99 Y66 K0

Wallpaper
1950s or 1960s

Unknown artist/maker

Screen-print on paper

UK

E.1465-2010
Given by Alastair and Anna Seagroatt-
Davidson, in memory of our dad, Michael
Edgar Howard Seagroatt, Liverpool 2010

This wallpaper piece is one of a group
of four unused samples acquired from
a house in Liverpool. Its colour scheme
and bold asymmetric floral pattern are
distinctively 1950s in style. Screen-printing,
a centuries-old craft technique, gradually
evolved into an industrial method in the
first half of the 20th century. As seen
in this example, slight irregularities or
idiosyncrasies in the design can appear
when the thin inks that are pushed
through the screen mesh are unevenly
applied or overlay each other.

C35 M58 Y73 K18

C1 M14 Y73 K0

C70 M79 Y56 K88

C3 M7 Y4 K0

C10 M75 Y99 K1

Calyx
Furnishing fabric
1951

Lucienne Day (1917–2010)
Screen-printed linen
UK

CIRC.190-1954

Created by Lucienne Day for the Festival of Britain in 1951, this innovative design, with its stylized plant motifs reminiscent of the art of Joan Miró and Paul Klee, and its combination of bright and muted colours, has had a lasting influence on textiles ever since. The fabric was produced by Heal's Wholesale and Export (the precursor of Heal Fabrics), which went on to work closely with Lucienne Day. This design won a gold medal at the Milan Triennale in 1951 and the International Award of the American Institute of Decorators for best textile design in 1952.

C42 M43 Y46 K6

C66 M64 Y60 K52

C43 M27 Y85 K4

C10 M12 Y14 K0

C16 M30 Y80 K0

Sans Souci
Furnishing fabric
*c.*1953

Hilda Durkin (fl.1950–60)
for Edinburgh Weavers

Printed cotton

UK

T.169-2009
Given by Sara Lee Courtaulds

This striking design is by Hilda Durkin,
a prominent 1950s freelance designer
whose name is not widely known today.
It was drawn in crayons and screen-printed
on cotton crêpe. Durkin created six other
designs for Edinburgh Weavers, all
characterized by similarly strong graphic
lines and fresh colours. Her clients also
included Liberty & Co., for whom she
designed the popular fabric *Isola Bella*.

C12 M11 Y17 K0

C58 M35 Y53 K8

C58 M45 Y59 K18

C58 M22 Y32 K1

C34 M85 Y69 K35

C69 M66 Y64 K69

Coppice
Furnishing fabric
1954

Mary White (b.1930) for Heal's
Printed cotton
UK

T.545:3-1999
Given by Heal & Son Ltd.

This versatile design with an abstract tree motif was reproduced by Heal's in a variety of colourways including a slate blue, dark blue, black, green and mauve palette; and another in black, brown, orange, yellow and blue. It was designed by Mary White, one of the most iconic and popular British textile designers of the 1950s. White also worked as a ceramicist and potter and started Thanet Pottery in 1961 with her brother David White. In 2008 her son and daughter-in-law revived some of her prints for a limited clothing range.

C51 M42 Y45 K7

C15 M34 Y44 K0

C66 M71 Y64 K83

C2 M3 Y7 K0

C5 M9 Y93 K0

C43 M22 Y1 K0

Raimoult
Furnishing fabric
1954

Robert Stewart (1924–95)
for Liberty & Co. Ltd

UK

CIRC.487-1954

Scottish designer and artist Robert Stewart
was a contemporary of Lucienne Day and
they had a mutual admiration for each
other's work. The abstract shapes of this
design are typical of their innovative work
in the 1950s. Influential as a pioneering
teacher of textiles at Glasgow School
of Art, Stewart created mural, ceramic
and tapestry designs as well as fine art.
Mirroring Lucienne Day's design relationship
with Heal's, Stewart produced many fabric
designs for Liberty, as well as for Pringle
and Donald Brothers in the 1950s.

C32 M98 Y100 K47

C9 M32 Y89 K0

C75 M68 Y67 K88

C3 M3 Y1 K0

C51 M10 Y67 K0

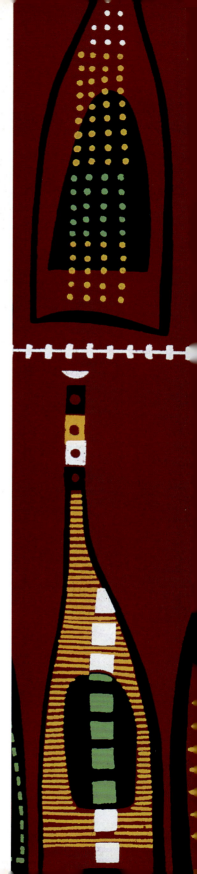

Malaga
Wallpaper
1955

Wallpaper Manufacturers Ltd
(Lightbown Aspinall branch)

Colour screen-print

UK

E.444:23-1988
Given by Arthur Sanderson & Sons Ltd

Wallpapers fell out of fashion during the period of Modernist architecture and design. The Palladio range by Wallpaper Manufacturers Ltd was designed in the 1950s to bring wallpaper back into the interiors of public and private modern buildings. The Palladio pattern *Malaga* was intended for cafés, coffee bars and restaurants, as well as for the domestic kitchen-diner. It reflects the new interest in holidays abroad and in foreign food and wine.

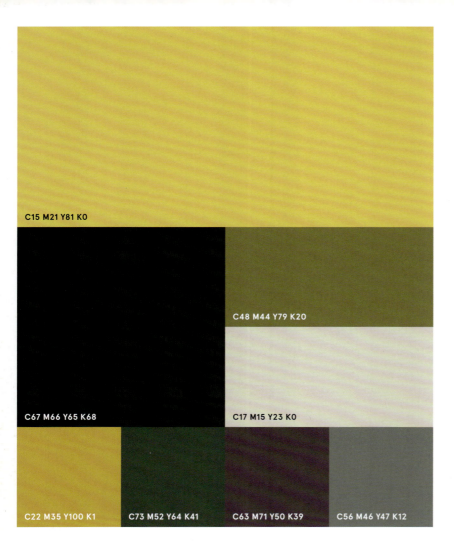

C15 M21 Y81 K0

C48 M44 Y79 K20

C67 M66 Y65 K68

C17 M15 Y23 K0

C22 M35 Y100 K1

C73 M52 Y64 K41

C63 M71 Y50 K39

C56 M46 Y47 K12

Mirage
Furnishing fabric
1955

Robert Stewart
for Liberty & Co. Ltd

Roller-printed cotton

UK

CIRC.677B-1956
Given by Liberty & Co

Liberty & Co. first commissioned Robert Stewart to design souvenir products for the 1951 Festival of Britain, and his work subsequently figured importantly in the company's strategy of modernizing their range. His textile designs for Liberty were never mass-produced, despite the obvious popular appeal of their aesthetic, and it is perhaps for this reason that they are less well known than those of his contemporary Lucienne Day. In recent years, however, his designs, including *Mirage* and *Raimoult* (see pages 218–19) have been reproduced and have proved enduringly popular.

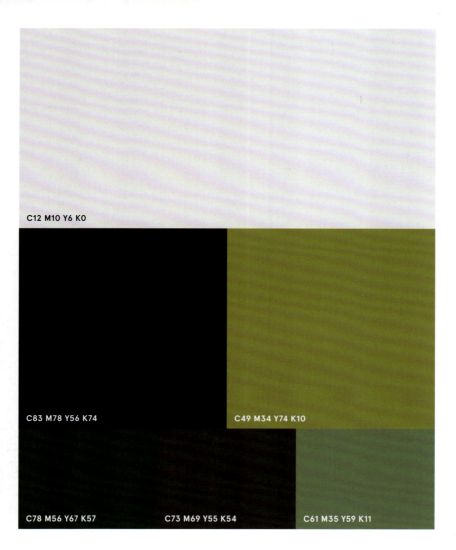

C12 M10 Y6 K0

C83 M78 Y56 K74

C49 M34 Y74 K10

C78 M56 Y67 K57

C73 M69 Y55 K54

C61 M35 Y59 K11

Pheasant Moon
Furnishing fabric
1960

Hans Tisdall (1910–97)
for Edinburgh Weavers

Screen-printed satin

UK

CIRC.6-1961
Given by Edinburgh Weavers

This dynamic furnishing fabric pattern has an enormous repeat of 220 cm (86.5 in.), and its printing process would have required several screens. It reflects the flamboyant style of its designer, Hans Tisdall. His designs for Edinburgh Weavers favour monumental motifs that retain elegance and delicacy of line, despite their size. A mural painter, as well as an illustrator and book jacket designer, Tisdall was an expert at creating both floor-to-ceiling designs and more small-scale works.

C79 M56 Y41 K19

C16 M19 Y20 K0

C29 M48 Y51 K3

C51 M36 Y22 K0

C27 M23 Y75 K1

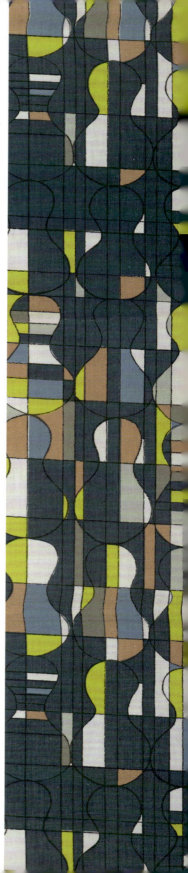

Melody
Furnishing fabric
1960s

Jacqueline Groag (1903–86)
for Edinburgh Weavers
Printed cotton
UK

T.55-2009
Given by Sara Lee Courtaulds

Influential Czech designer Jacqueline Groag designed textiles for the Wiener Werkstätte and unique hand-printed fabrics for leading Parisian fashion houses including Chanel, Schiaparelli and Lanvin, before coming to the UK in 1939. Her work featured in the 1951 Festival of Britain and was very much in the 'Festival' or 'Contemporary' spirit, described at the time as 'clean, fresh and new'. *Melody*, designed for Edinburgh Weavers, is similarly fresh and has a fragmented yet harmonious composition.

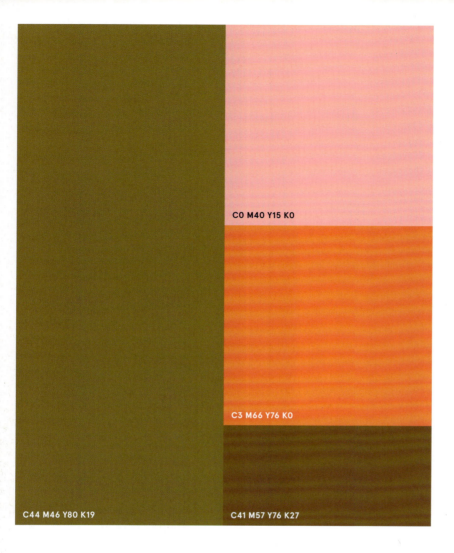

C0 M40 Y15 K0

C3 M66 Y76 K0

C44 M46 Y80 K19

C41 M57 Y76 K27

Rhapsody
Furnishing fabric
1964

Michael Griffin (fl.1960s) for Heal
Fabrics Ltd

Machine screen-printed
cotton crêpe

UK

CIRC.751-1964
Given by Heal Fabrics Ltd.

This fabric is entirely characteristic of
1960s surface design, with its flat, stylized
floral motifs and muted yet clashing colour
scheme of olive green and salmon pink.
The Pop aesthetic of the time was based
on saturated colours and unashamedly
bold motifs. Heal Fabrics mass-produced
this machine screen-printed furnishing
fabric and marketed it as 'shrink resist'.

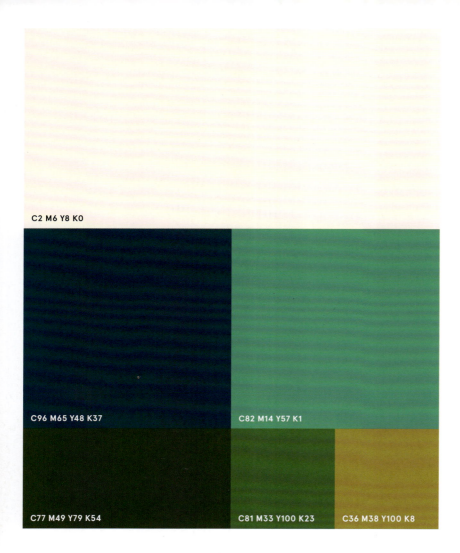

C2 M6 Y8 K0

C96 M65 Y48 K37

C82 M14 Y57 K1

C77 M49 Y79 K54

C81 M33 Y100 K23

C36 M38 Y100 K8

Lahore
Furnishing fabric
1968

Sushil Datta (b.1938)
for Edinburgh Weavers

Printed textile

UK

T.18.1 to 3-2009
Given by Sara Lee Courtaulds

This fabric reflects the late 1960s and '70s fashion in Britain for Indian and Indian-inspired motifs and designs. It was created for Edinburgh Weavers by Sushil Datta, who was born in the part of India that is now Bangladesh. Datta's intricate and vivid designs for wallpapers and fabrics were commissioned by several other clients including Liberty & Co., Sanderson, John Lewis and Cole & Sons.

C84 M76 Y49 K49

C21 M88 Y96 K12

C31 M64 Y28 K1

C81 M56 Y51 K31

Jardin
Wallpaper
1968

Tony Fraser (fl.1968–74) for
Sanderson
Silkscreen print, on paper
UK

E.5164-1968
Given by Wallpaper Manufacturers Ltd

The simplified motifs, bold outlines
and vibrant colours found in 1960s fabric
designs were influenced by print-based
Pop art, and lent themselves equally
well to wallpaper prints like this example.
Tony Fraser's abstract interpretation of
a floral garden breaks confidently with
a long tradition of more naturalistic
floral wallpaper patterns. This sample
comes from a pattern book produced
by Sanderson-Rigg of Bridlington
for Sanderson.

C88 M64 Y0 K0

C40 M0 Y80 K0

C12 M10 Y9 K0

C24 M100 Y100 K19

C48 M4 Y24 K0

C85 M36 Y100 K31

Design for a textile
*c.*1970

Mary Yonge (1908–2010)
Watercolour, pencil and ink
on paper
UK

E.245-2011
Given by Eileen Knowles

Mary Yonge worked for many years as a textile designer for Courtaulds before becoming the Head of Studio. While she was working at Courtaulds, Yonge taught one day a week at the Central School of Arts and Design, where she had been a student. Yonge retired from Courtaulds and began working freelance in the 1960s. During this period she worked with a group that sold designs to major companies including Liberty & Co. and Edinburgh Weavers.

C71 M69 Y63 K75

C47 M42 Y70 K15

C74 M46 Y75 K41

C49 M78 Y68 K68

C27 M45 Y29 K0

C59 M40 Y23 K1

C13 M24 Y37 K0

C33 M11 Y24 K0

C77 M54 Y47 K24

C33 M68 Y100 K27

C58 M75 Y45 K31

C28 M40 Y66 K3

Cottage Garden
Furnishing fabric
1974

Susan Collier (1938–2011) & Sarah
Campbell (b.1946) for Liberty &
Co. Ltd

Screen-printed cotton

UK

T.44-1978

British design partnership Collier Campbell
began in the 1960s after Susan Collier sold
six designs to Liberty & Co. and set up a
freelance design studio with her sister,
Sarah Campbell. Their designs introduced
new colour palettes, often inspired
by contemporary fashion, into interior
furnishings. *Cottage Garden*, painted after
a visit to the Chelsea Flower Show, was
intended as naturalistic floral 'in contrast
to the W. Morris look and the stylized
Lucienne Day'. According to Campbell,
this colourway was meant to evoke
'that dusky, soft lavender and eucalyptus
evening feeling', with a dark ground
'to emphasize the density of the garden'.

C4 M6 Y4 K0

C69 M62 Y61 K54

C12 M5 Y100 K0

C58 M0 Y94 K0

C0 M62 Y99 K0

C71 M27 Y0 K0

C100 M16 Y33 K1

April
Design for
a wallpaper
1976

Jacqueline Groag
Collage and poster-colour over
dye-line print
UK

E.944-1978

Czech-born Jacqueline Groag's prolific
career spanned seven decades, and
yet her style always appeared modern.
Her work testifies to her knowledge
of art history and her sharp eye for
contemporary fashion. This hand-drawn
geometric wallpaper design, created
in the 1970s, shows her typically sparing
yet effective use of bright colours.

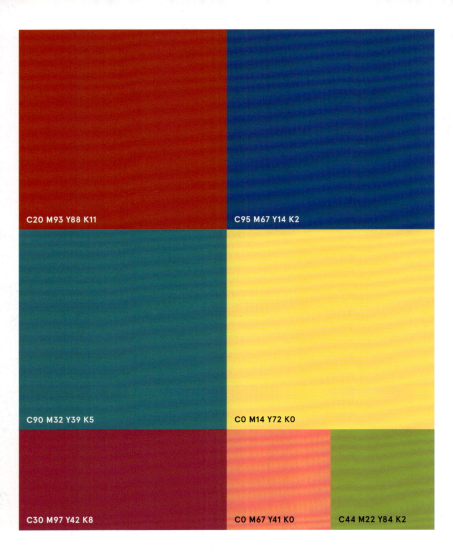

C20 M93 Y88 K11

C95 M67 Y14 K2

C90 M32 Y39 K5

C0 M14 Y72 K0

C30 M97 Y42 K8

C0 M67 Y41 K0

C44 M22 Y84 K2

Butterflies
Design for a textile
1981

Susan Collier & Sarah Campbell
Pencil and bodycolour
UK

E.265-1984
Given by Susan Collier

The painterly sensibility and freedom that Susan Collier and Sarah Campbell brought to textile design can be clearly seen in this joyously colourful painting for a dress fabric. They hand-painted all their designs, avoiding mechanical or computer processes, to achieve rich, lively variations in colour and line. Collier's motto was said to be 'cheat the repeat.' This free-looking pattern nevertheless has a subtle, careful regularity, explains Campbell: 'There is a mix of organic and seemingly abstract shapes, all emanating from butterflies, leaves, fruits, tendrils, etc; the whole is held together by the balance of the colours and the consistency of the marks.'

C68 M53 Y33 K9

C48 M37 Y30 K1

C33 M27 Y34 K0

C28 M100 Y42 K8

C15 M85 Y100 K5

C99 M86 Y0 K0

C18 M29 Y100 K1

C76 M69 Y63 K77

Pharo
Furnishing fabric
1986

Habitat
Printed fabric
UK

T.135–1986
Given by Habitat

The name of this printed furnishing fabric, *Pharo* (a phonetic spelling of 'pharaoh'), appears to indicate the source of the motifs, with its stripes of hot orange and pink, sunny yellow and Mediterranean blue set against a muted background of pyramids. This textile was sold by British firm Habitat from 1986.

C5 M3 Y21 K0

C0 M11 Y84 K0

C67 M45 Y98 K40

C8 M57 Y43 K0

C90 M50 Y56 K32

C26 M14 Y97 K0

C94 M76 Y38 K26

C23 M69 Y100 K11

Tracer
Furnishing fabric
1992

Michael Heindorff (b.1949)
for Designers Guild

Screen-printed cotton

UK

T.428:3-1992
Given by Designers Guild

Designers Guild was founded in 1970 by Robin and Tricia Guild. Tricia Guild and designer Chris Halsey produced their first range of textiles based on a collection of Indian hand-printed fabrics in November 1971. In 1992, artist Michael Heindorff was commissioned to create a fabric range. The textiles in the resulting 'Still Life Collection', according to Heindorff, 'all share their reference in design and name to nature … The palette is akin to the colours in many of my paintings, as are translucency and tone.' *Tracer*, made in three different colourways, is typical of the abstract designs and bright, acid colours favoured by Designers Guild.

20TH–21ST CENTURY

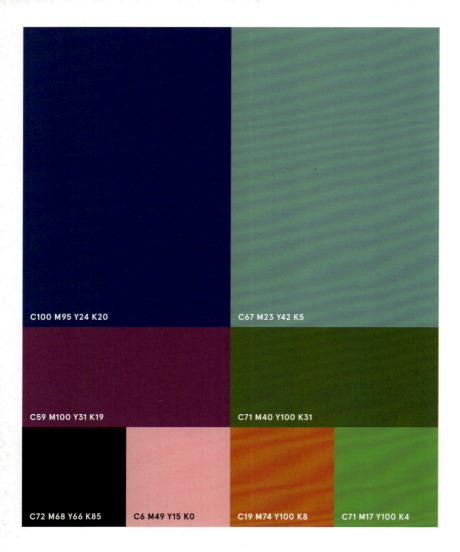

C100 M95 Y24 K20

C67 M23 Y42 K5

C59 M100 Y31 K19

C71 M40 Y100 K31

C72 M68 Y66 K85

C6 M49 Y15 K0

C19 M74 Y100 K8

C71 M17 Y100 K4

Large Eel
**Furnishing fabric
1992**

Paul Simmons (b.1967)
for Timorous Beasties
Screen-printed cotton velvet
UK

T.422-1992

Timorous Beasties was established in
1990 by Paul Simmons and Alistair McAuley,
who met while studying textile design at
the Glasgow School of Art. Their early
printed designs were characterized by
vivid colours and dramatic large-scale
flora and fauna derived from illustrated
encyclopaedias. Simmons and McAuley's
style has been described as 'William
Morris on acid' — iconoclastic, yet also
informed by their deep knowledge of
the history of textiles.

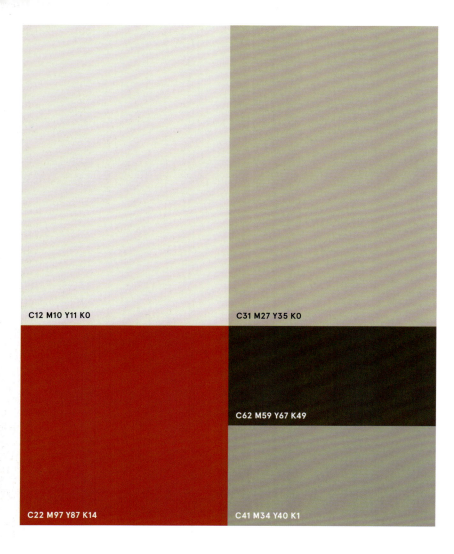

C12 M10 Y11 K0

C31 M27 Y35 K0

C62 M59 Y67 K49

C22 M97 Y87 K14

C41 M34 Y40 K1

Mademoiselle
Furnishing fabric
2000

Celia Birtwell (b.1941)
Printed cotton twill
UK

T.21-2008
Given by Celia Birtwell

Internationally acclaimed British textile designer Celia Birtwell has been described as '1960s textile print icon'. In 1966 she collaborated with Ossie Clark on a fashion collection for the Quorum boutique in London. Their subsequent work produced a style that has become inextricably linked with the Swinging Sixties. In 1984, Birtwell opened her own shop in London's Bayswater, where she diversified into furnishing fabrics. This fabric features a Victorian-inspired striped 'wallpaper' background decorated with red and black printed 'pictures' of women and flowers in oval frames.

C15 M13 Y16 K0

C10 M18 Y81 K0

C22 M47 Y46 K1

C55 M50 Y44 K12

C57 M24 Y80 K5

C13 M65 Y100 K2

C40 M70 Y54 K21

Flower Bed
Wallpaper
2003

Trenton Doyle Hancock (b.1974)
Screenprint on vinyl-coated paper
USA

E.15-2015
Given by James Cohan Gallery

American artist Trenton Doyle Hancock draws on the history of painting and pop culture to build extensive, fantastical narratives. This *Flower Bed* wallpaper, forming part of Hancock's unfolding story, reflects a character's obsession with his flower garden (which ultimately becomes a sexual obsession) and his wife's anger at this betrayal.

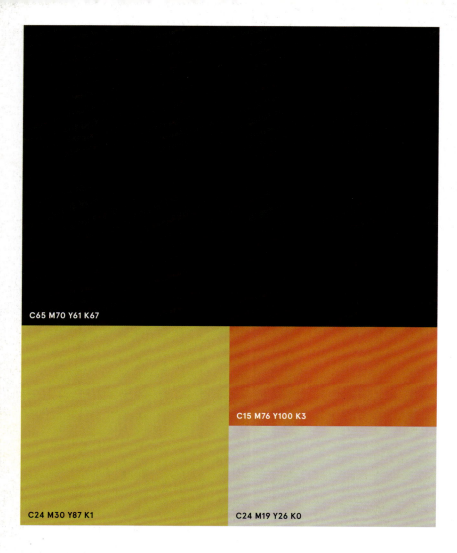

C65 M70 Y61 K67

C15 M76 Y100 K3

C24 M30 Y87 K1

C24 M19 Y26 K0

Brilliant Me
Wallpaper
2009

De Angelis & Garner
Surface print on paper
UK

E.1406–2010
Given by De Angelis & Garner

Artist and designer Marchella De Angelis
and photographer Kate Garner began
collaborating in 2006 to produce bespoke
wallpapers. Many of the designs are
derived from photographs by Garner,
including this wallpaper, which is based
on Garner's pictures of influential punk/
New Romantic performance artist and
queer icon Leigh Bowery (1961–94).
An image of Bowery's boldly made-up
face has been metamorphosed into vivid
orchid-like flower motifs. The design
is printed in colourways that reference
1970s styles.

Further reading

Find out more about the V&A objects featured in this book at www.vam.ac.uk. Search the collection for a specific pattern by using the museum number listed in the caption.

Baty, Patrick, *The Anatomy of Colour: The Story of Heritage Paints and Pigments* (London and New York 2017)

Brodie, Antonia, *V&A Pattern: Garden Florals* (London 2010)

Buruma, Anna, *Liberty & Co* (London 2012)

Beddard, Honor, and Douglas Dodds, *V&A Pattern: Digital Pioneers* (London 2009)

Chang, Yueh-Siang, *V&A Pattern: Chinese Textiles* (London 2010)

Crill, Rosemary, *V&A Pattern: Indian Florals* (London 2009)

Crill, Rosemary (ed.), *The Fabric of India* (London 2015)

Cullen, Oriole, *V&A Pattern: Pop Patterns* (London 2011)

Day, Susan, *Carpets of the Art Deco Era* (London and New York 2015)

Grant, Sarah, *Toiles de Jouy: French Printed Cottons* (London 2010)

Hawksley, Lucinda, *Bitten By Witch Fever: Wallpaper and Arsenic in the Victorian Home* (London and New York 2016)

Hefford, Wendy, *The Victoria and Albert Musuem's Textile Collection: Design for Printed Textiles in England from 1750 to 1850* (London 1992)

Jackson, Anna, *V&A Pattern: Kimono* (London 2010)

Jackson, Lesley, *Alastair Morton and Edinburgh Weavers: Visionary Textiles and Modern Art* (London 2012)

Leslie, Fiona, *Designs for 20th-Century Interiors* (London 2000)

Livingstone, Karen, *V&A Pattern: C.F.A. Voysey* (London 2013)

Livingstone, Karen, Max Donnelly and Linda Parry, *C.F.A. Voysey: Arts & Crafts Designer* (London 2016)

Massey, Anne, *Interior Design Since 1900 (World of Art series)* (London and New York 2008)

Miller, Lesley Ellis, *Selling Silks: A Merchant's Sample Book 1764* (London 2014)

Mendes, Valerie D., *V&A Pattern: Novelty Patterns* (London 2010)

Parry, Linda (ed.), *William Morris Textiles* (London 2013)

Parry, Linda (ed.), *British Textiles: 1700 to the Present* (London 2010)

Parry, Linda, *V&A Pattern: William Morris* (London 2009)

Praz, Mario, and William Weaver, *An Illustrated History of Interior Decoration: From Pompeii to Art Nouveau* (London and New York 1982)

Pritchard, Sue, *V&A Pattern: The Fifties* (London 2009)

Saunders, Gill, *Wallpaper in Interior Decoration* (London and New York 2002)

Schoeser, Mary, *Sanderson: The Essence of English Decoration* (London and New York 2010)

Schoeser, Mary, *V&A Pattern: Heal's* (London 2012)

Schoeser, Mary, *V&A Pattern: Sanderson 1954–74* (London 2012)

Thomas, Abraham, *V&A Pattern: Owen Jones* (London 2010)

Thunder, Moira, *V&A Pattern: Spitalfield Silks* (London 2011)

Wearden, Jennifer, and Patricia L. Baker, *Iranian Textiles* (London 2010)

Whitake, Esmé, *V&A Pattern: Walter Crane* (London 2011)

Wilson, Verity, *Chinese Textiles* (London 2005)

Acknowledgments

With thanks to everyone who made up the palette for this book:

The team at Here Design, especially to Camille Blais for the original idea and the design of this book; Caz Hildebrand, Kara Johnson, Tom Key, Tom Bacon and Alex Merrett.

The team at Thames & Hudson Ltd, London: Julian Honer, Susannah Lawson, Tamara Stanton, Luke Kiley, Rachel Heley and Flora Spiegel.

The editors and curators at the Victoria and Albert Museum, for help with sourcing images, information and research: Kathryn Johnson, Coralie Hepburn, Hannah Newell, Gill Saunders and Amelia Calver.

Picture credits

On the cover: Wallpaper by unknown artist/maker, 1950s or 1960s
screen-print on paper, UK (see pages 210–11)

First published in the United Kingdom in 2018 by Thames & Hudson Ltd,
London, in association with the Victoria and Albert Museum.

Spectrum: Heritage Patterns and Colours © 2018 Victoria and Albert
Museum/Thames & Hudson Ltd, London

Text and V&A photographs © 2018 Victoria and Albert Museum, London

Introduction by Ros Byam Shaw © 2018 Victoria and Albert
Museum, London

Design © 2018 Thames & Hudson Ltd, London

Designed by Camille Blais for Here Design

British Library Cataloguing-in-Publication Data

A catalogue record for this book is available from the British Library

ISBN 978-0-500-48026-7

Printed and bound in China by C & C Offset Printing Co. Ltd

To find out about all our publications, please visit
www.thamesandhudson.com. There you can subscribe
to our e-newsletter, browse or download our current
catalogue, and buy any titles that are in print.

V&A Publishing

Supporting the world's leading
museum of art and design,
the Victoria and Albert
Museum, London